NoW DEAD IS WHAT WE MAY LEARN FROM THEIR

DESTROYED NoW WHAT WoULD FUTURE CIVILIZA-

THEY MEAN ToDAY AND ToMoRRoW IS IMPORTANT

IOST OF THESE WILL STAND 3oo YEARS AT LEAST,

LIVING ARCHITECTURE" EXHIBITION, 1951

"WE HAVE RUINED MORE, WASTED MORE,
TRAMPLED ON MORE THAN ANY CIVILIZATION
THE WoRLD HAS EVER SEEN—IN A SHORTER
TIME Too."

FRANK LLOYD WRIGHT
LECTURE To STUDENTS, 1950

LOST WRIGHT

FRANK LLOYD WRIGHT'S VANISHED MASTERPIECES

CARLA LIND

AN ARCHETYPE PRESS BOOK

SIMON & SCHUSTER EDITIONS

SIMON & SCHUSTER EDITIONS
Rockefeller Center
1230 Avenue of the Americas
New York, NY 10020

Dedicated to John Lind

Produced by Archetype Press, Inc., Washington, D.C.

Project Director: Diane Maddex

Designer: Robert L. Wiser

Editor: Gretchen Smith Mui

Editorial Assistant: Kristi Flis

Printed in Hong Kong

1   3   5   7   9   10   8   6   4   2

Library of Congress Cataloging-in-Publication Data

Lind, Carla.

Lost Wright : Frank Lloyd Wright's vanished masterpieces / Carla Lind.

        p.   cm.

"An Archetype Press book."

Includes bibliographical references and index.

1. Wright, Frank Lloyd, 1867–1959 — Criticism and interpretation. 2. Lost architecture — United States. 3. Organic architecture — United States. I. Title.

NA737.W7L55   1996

720´.92—dc20   96-15462

ISBN 0-684-81306-8

Opening illustrations: Page 1, Frank Lloyd Wright with Olgivanna, Iovanna, and Svetlana in 1929 at Ocatilla in Arizona. Pages 2–3, Watercolor of Ocatilla by George Kastner. Pages 4–5, Wright's drawing of the Larkin Administration Building in Buffalo, New York. Pages 6–7, Midway Gardens, Wright's entertainment complex in Chicago.

Chapter opener illustrations: Pages 16–17, Taliesin I. Pages 38–39, Little house II. Pages 74–75, Francis Apartments. Pages 82–83, Conservatory, Darwin Martin house. Pages 98–99, Delavan Lake Yacht Club. Pages 132–33, Larkin Administration Building. Pages 148–49, Usonian Exhibition Pavilion. Pages 162–63, Joseph Bagley house. Pages 168–69, Barnsdall Little Dipper.

CoNTENTS

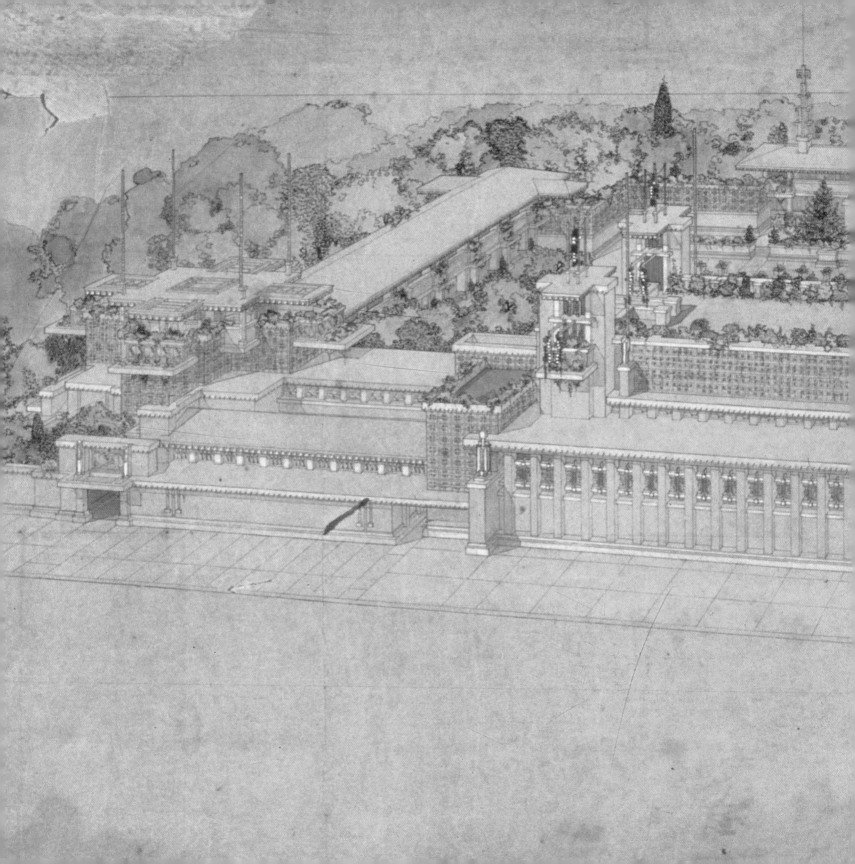

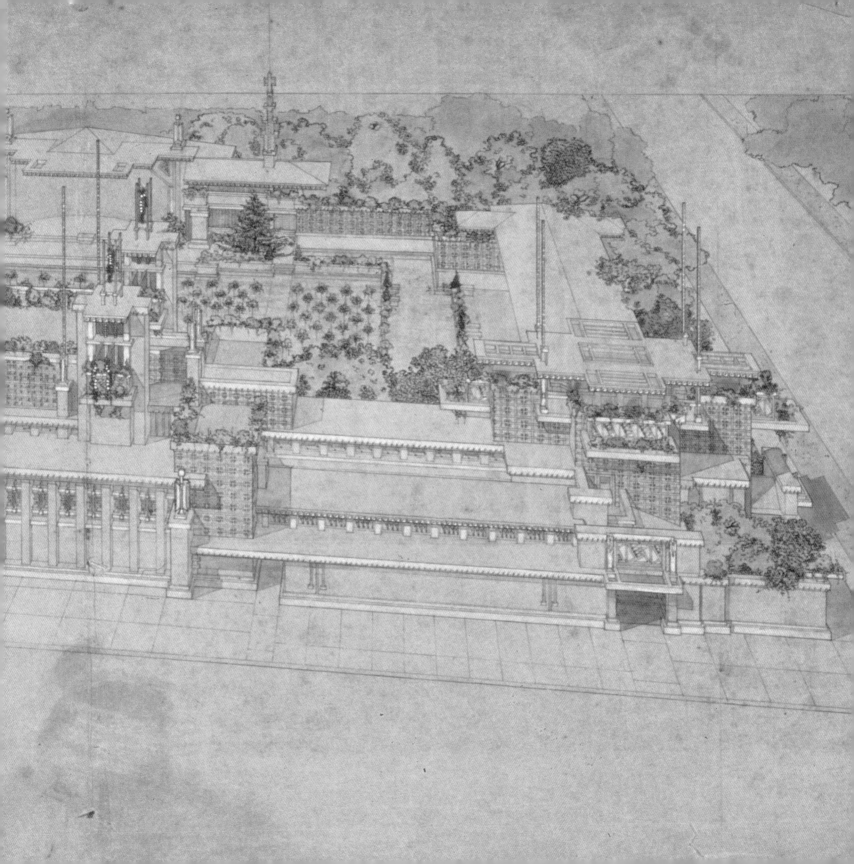

CHRONOLOGY

1856

Richard and Mary Lloyd Jones, Frank Lloyd Wright's maternal grandparents, settle in the Wisconsin River valley, where the family eventually owns 1,800 acres.

1867

Anna Lloyd Jones, twenty-seven, a teacher, marries William Russell Carey Wright, forty-one, a Baptist minister and musician.

1867

Frank Lloyd Wright is born on June 8 in Richland Center, Wisconsin, the first of the Wrights' three children.

1876

At the Philadelphia Centennial Exposition Anna purchases Froebel blocks for Frank, which impart a lifelong fascination with geometric shapes and systems.

1879

After moving from church to church around the country, the Wrights relocate to Madison, Wisconsin, where William opens a music conservatory. Frank spends summers on his uncles' farms.

1884

William and Anna divorce, after which Frank never sees his father again.

1886

Frank enters the University of Wisconsin as a civil engineering student and works as a junior draftsman.

1887

Wright is employed in Chicago by Joseph Lyman Silsbee, the architect for his uncle's church.

1888–93

Wright works for Adler and Sullivan until he is found to be designing "bootleg" houses on his own.

1889

Frank, twenty-two, marries Catherine Lee Tobin, eighteen, whom he met at his uncle's church, and designs a home for them in the Chicago suburb of Oak Park.

1890

Frank Lloyd Wright Jr., the first of their six children, is born.

1893

The young architect opens his own practice in Chicago's Steinway Hall.

1895

The Wrights' Oak Park home is modified with a new playroom.

1898

A studio addition unites Wright's personal and professional life as his practice thrives.

1900

Wright designs his first Prairie Style house.

1905

Frank and Catherine make their first trip to Japan, sailing with their clients the Willetses.

1907

The Art Institute of Chicago gives Wright his first solo exhibition.

1908

Wright publishes "In the Cause of Architecture," a comprehensive statement of his theories, in *Architectural Record*.

1909

Wright sails for Europe with his lover and client, Mamah Borthwick Cheney, leaving his wife of twenty years and six children aged six to nineteen. He works on his *Ausgeführte Bauten und Entwürfe,* which is published by Wasmuth in Germany in 1910.

1911
Wright builds the first Taliesin, his retreat near Spring Green, Wisconsin.

1913
The Midway Gardens and Imperial Hotel commissions begin.

1914
Mamah Borthwick Cheney, her two children, and four others are murdered at Taliesin by an employee who also sets fire to the house.

1915
Miriam Noel, who will become Wright's second wife, moves to Taliesin.

1916–22
Wright spends most of his time in Tokyo working on the Imperial Hotel.

1923
Anna Lloyd Wright dies. Catherine divorces Frank fourteen years after their separation, and he marries Miriam Noel in December. They separate six months later.

1923–25
Wright briefly establishes an office in California and completes five commissions, four using the textile-block method that his son Lloyd supervises.

1925
Wright, then fifty-eight, meets Olga Ivanovna (Olgivanna) Lazovich Hinzenberg, twenty-seven, a Gurdijieff dancer. She and her eight-year-old daughter, Svetlana, move into Taliesin. Their daughter, Iovanna, is born. Another fire strikes Taliesin.

1927
Wright divorces Noel after a three-year separation, becomes incorporated to settle his financial problems, and begins his autobiography.

1928
Wright marries Olgivanna.

1930
Wright's Kahn Lectures at Princeton sum up forty years of his architectural ideas.

1932
Wright's first autobiography is published (revised in 1943), and he and Olgivanna establish the Taliesin Fellowship.

1935–36
The Fallingwater and Johnson Wax commissions breathe new life into his career. Wright designs his first Usonian house and builds the Broadacre City model.

1937
Work begins on Taliesin West, Wright's winter home in Arizona.

1949
Wright receives the AIA Gold Medal for Architecture, one of numerous awards and honorary degrees.

1950s
Among many residential and public buildings, Wright designs the Guggenheim Museum in New York City.

1951
The exhibition *Frank Lloyd Wright: Sixty Years of Living Architecture* opens in Philadelphia and then tours the world, returning to New York in 1953.

1958
Wright publishes *The Living City,* his last book, about Broadacre City.

1959
Wright dies two months before his ninety-second birthday.

1985
Olgivanna Wright dies.

INTRODUCTION

How could it happen, we ask? How could buildings by Frank Lloyd Wright, America's most celebrated architect, be destroyed? Our disbelief in the face of such a tragedy is testimony to the increased outrage that occurs when significant historic buildings are demolished. Realistically, we know that all buildings are doomed to perish, their elements returned to the earth of which they were made. Yet some losses are premature and decidedly more tragic than others. All designs of a great master such as Wright take on increased meaning because they are part of his or her body of work and hold information about the person's time and accomplishments and the work of others who preceded and followed it.

Frank Lloyd Wright's seventy-year career yielded more than one thousand designs (not all of them built). His practice began in Chicago in 1887 and, like many young careers, grew in concentric circles that reflected his relationships. Early clients were those he met through his family, in the office of his employers, and in his neighborhood of Oak Park, Illinois. Wright's uncanny ability to recover from setbacks, to soar in the face of disaster, and to keep his message alive was Olympian. When he died in 1959 he left roughly five hundred revolutionary buildings in thirty-six states and two foreign countries and had been honored worldwide. In addition to his architectural practice, he was a prolific writer and lecturer and operated his own school, the Taliesin Fellowship, which was based at his two homes in Spring Green, Wisconsin, and Scottsdale, Arizona.

Wright's basic tenets of organic architecture, which he had formulated by the turn of the twentieth century, endured throughout his career. Their manifestations seemed endless—whether in the Prairie Style, in concrete textile blocks, in Usonian houses, or in something in between. Each creation upset the architectural status quo one more time. No borrowed styles for him: Wright's buildings looked at life's problems afresh. Agricultural specialists studied his farm buildings just as social commentators and critics looked at his solutions for housing the American family.

Yet 118 Wright-designed buildings, including individual structures that were part of multiple-building projects, are now gone—a full twenty percent of the architect's built work. These lost structures are amazingly representative of his career, from early to late, from coast to coast, from poultry shed to

At the exhibition *Frank Lloyd Wright: Sixty Years of Living Architecture*, held in 1953 on the site of the Guggenheim Museum in New York City, Frank Lloyd Wright paused to contemplate photomurals of his recently razed Larkin Administration Building (1903) in Buffalo, New York.

corporate headquarters, from rural lakeside to urban center. Significant portions of seventeen others have also vanished.

Granted, some commissions—such as exhibitions and tent structures in the Arizona desert—were designed to be temporary, but most were not. Their vulnerability was particularly affected by their intended use: camps and some recreation buildings were seasonal and less expensively built, commercial interiors were redecorated. And of course natural disasters occur. Thirty-one Wright structures were lost to fire, one to an earthquake, and one to a hurricane. Time ate away others. Solidly built houses and businesses that could have endured for decades, however, were also demolished. The only sure protection may have been divine. Of the nine Wright churches that were built, all still stand. The greatest predators, of course, have been human, spurred variously by economics, fashion, and utility.

Fortunately, in the past two decades only four Wright buildings have been lost. Awareness helps, and the attention given to the Wright oeuvre in recent years has been phenomenal. But many important buildings, Wrightian and non-Wrightian, are still threatened every day. Why? Usually because of money, or the lack of it, and expediency—both driving forces in our society. As the late Chicago photographer and preservationist Richard Nickel observed, "Money built the buildings, and money will destroy them."

It is difficult to stand in another person's shoes in another time and try to second-guess a decision to demolish a building. Land values change. Needs change. Dreams become disappointments. Commercial development encroaches on some residential neighborhoods, while others decline. Tastes evolve, leaving buildings vacant and furnishings discarded. Buildings recognized as revolutionary by some are considered odd by others.

There are two ways of discouraging needless loss: recognition and regular maintenance. If a building is accepted as being significant, remains useful, and has economic value, it will survive longer. Deferred maintenance leads to a building's diminishment and allows it to gradually become unimportant. Neglect makes a structure vulnerable to natural forces, gives owners, developers, and governments reasons to demolish, and softens the resolve of protesting citizens.

Total loss, however, is not the only issue. Partial loss of Wright's multi-

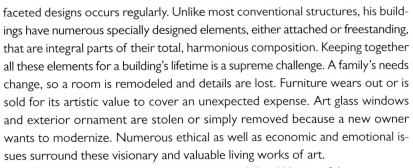

faceted designs occurs regularly. Unlike most conventional structures, his buildings have numerous specially designed elements, either attached or freestanding, that are integral parts of their total, harmonious composition. Keeping together all these elements for a building's lifetime is a supreme challenge. A family's needs change, so a room is remodeled and details are lost. Furniture wears out or is sold for its artistic value to cover an unexpected expense. Art glass windows and exterior ornament are stolen or simply removed because a new owner wants to modernize. Numerous ethical as well as economic and emotional issues surround these visionary and valuable living works of art.

We live in a world of limited resources and should be careful not to waste the buildings that exist. Preventing the needless loss of significant buildings, whether by gradual deterioration, alteration, or sudden demolition, begins with awareness. Once buildings are identified and named, they become—like birds, flowers, and constellations—more treasured. Although we cannot be sure of how Wright would have viewed the loss or threatened loss of his works, his opposition to the proposed demolition in the 1950s of the Robie house (1906) in Chicago puts him on record as a preservationist. We do know, however, that his own homes changed continuously—nothing was sacred, and losses presented new challenges. But preservation is for others to decide. Retaining a record of civilization's achievements, of the contributions of our innovators, is important to all humankind.

How do we who care about these treasures respond to potential losses? Some protest, seeking legal and political solutions. Others salvage remnants and mount them like stuffed heads as reminders of a building that once had life. Some document with photographs or measured drawings. Some save and reconstruct portions of buildings as rooms in museums. Others write about them to keep the idea alive. Whichever path we choose, it is imperative that when we see the need, we do something besides shake our heads.

Each state now has a designated state historic preservation office in the state capital that serves as a liaison with the National Park Service, the federal government's key preservation agency. A list of these is available by calling 202-343-5726. These offices can provide technical assistance as well as information about adding a property or historic district to the National Register of Historic Places. The National Trust for Historic Preservation (202-673-4000)

13

An electrical fire destroyed the top floor of Wright's Moore house (1895) in 1923. Originally Elizabethan in design, the Oak Park, Illinois, residence was reworked by Wright with bolder, more Mayan features and still stands in this Chicago suburb.

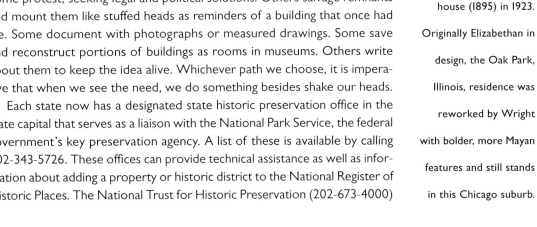

has regional offices that serve those interested in protecting significant buildings and sites. The Frank Lloyd Wright Building Conservancy (312-663-1683) in Chicago was formed specifically to aid in the preservation of Wright's work. But this is only a beginning.

A program of protection, encouragement, education, interpretation, and advocacy at the local level must follow. The real work of preservation begins in the schools and neighborhoods, with information programs, committees, ordinances, and districts that create a community attitude about important buildings and what they contribute to people's lives.

Determining just which Wright buildings have been lost began first with the confirmation that they were his and that they were in fact built. This seems simple enough, but a definitive list was sometimes elusive (see Other Works). The authorship of some buildings is in question, while others have gone unnoticed or were partially destroyed. Some were rebuilt. In multiple-building complexes, some units have been demolished, but others are intact.

The lost and altered buildings of Frank Lloyd Wright have been grouped into categories on the following pages to allow comparisons with similar works and then arranged generally chronologically. So much can be learned from these long-gone and sometimes forgotten works that they could have been categorized in countless ways.

Although more than one hundred distinctive creations of America's most famous architect have been lost, four times as many remain, often struggling to maintain viability. We can learn from our mistakes and cherish what we have. Wright's buildings have proven their relevance. Informal, environmentally sensitive, and based on a close relationship with the earth, these masterworks demand our respect along with our care.

Wright's famed Imperial Hotel (1915–23) in Tokyo survived a 1923 earthquake but not the pressures of rising urban land values. It was torn down in 1968 to make way for a modern high-rise hotel.

WRIGHT'S
PROPERTIES

Spaces under Frank Lloyd Wright's control—his own homes and properties as well as those he rented—were always in a state of flux and most susceptible to loss. During his life nearly continuous changes were made in response to new artistic inspiration or the evolving needs of his family and the Taliesin Fellowship, the group of apprentices who studied and resided with him. The places where he lived and worked were living organisms, responding to the conditions they encountered. Wright was in fact his own biggest client. Using his homes as laboratories, he experimented and experimented and experimented. Each place he lived after he left Oak Park in 1909 was not just his home but a complex of buildings designed to accommodate the needs of a community of individuals who lived and worked together. During his last twenty-seven years, Wright's fondness for change was facilitated by the existence of the Fellowship, which provided a steady pool of cheap labor eager to "learn by doing."

Not all changes were voluntary. Fire, which seemed to plague Wright throughout his long life, ravaged his Wisconsin home, Taliesin (1911–59) (left), three times. After each disaster he responded defiantly to the challenge and seized the opportunity to create yet another imaginative space for his own use. Rather than melting his spirit, fire seemed to temper his steel.

Only major changes to Wright's properties—those that resulted in the loss of an entire structure or wing—are presented here. Omitted are a number of small utility structures at Taliesin that deteriorated or became obsolete and were subsequently torn down; these include an old wash house, a machine shed, pig pens, and the carriage house behind Tanyderi, the home of Wright's sister Jane Porter. Although some spaces had outlived their usefulness and were simply eliminated, others were replaced with new designs. By tracking the buildings that were discarded by Wright or otherwise destroyed, it is possible to get a closer, behind-the-scenes look at the life of this inventive architect as he met the challenges of a vital yet turbulent seventy-year career. For one whose life and work were synonymous, the fallen buildings left in Wright's personal wake begin to tell his story.

HILLSIDE HOME SCHOOL I

Wright's aunts, the innovative educators Nell and Jane Lloyd Jones, retained their twenty-year-old nephew in 1887 to design this school, which they established on their parents' homestead. The progressive boarding school was rooted in the lessons of nature and was open to boys and girls. Many years later Wright's two oldest sons would attend Hillside Home, making the two-hundred-mile journey from their home in Oak Park, Illinois, on horseback.

The building's design drew on the work of the Chicago architect Joseph Lyman Silsbee, who had been commissioned the same year by Wright's uncle, the prominent Rev. Jenkin Lloyd Jones, to design his All Souls Church in Chicago as well as the family chapel (1886) in Spring Green. Wright had supervised the chapel's construction and would eventually work for Silsbee when he moved to Chicago. The Shingle Style, which Silsbee brought to the Midwest from the East, appealed to the transcendental aesthetics of the Lloyd Jones clan and became the basis for Wright's own first home in Oak Park (1889–98).

In 1902 Wright designed another school building with classrooms and a gymnasium, but his aunts continued to live in the older building. When the school closed in 1915, Wright took over the property, allowing the aunts and his mother, Anna Lloyd Wright, to live there if they wished, but it was mostly abandoned.

After their deaths Wright repeatedly tried to alter the original shingled school to fit the Prairie Style profile of his newer building. The Victorian wainscoted rooms were converted into several apartments, connected by a bridge to the main building, and used by young Taliesin apprentices in the 1940s. Wright had the shingles removed and the roof flattened and, awaiting an inspired solution, left it covered with tar paper for many years. But it was just too tall. Finally, it became an unbearable eyesore, and in 1950 he had it demolished, the fine oak flooring recycled into dining tables and shelving.

18

Taliesin

Highway 23

at Hillside School Road

Spring Green,

Wisconsin

Designed in 1887

Demolished in 1950

TALIESIN I

Seeking to begin a new chapter in his life, Wright left his family in Oak Park in 1909 and resided in Europe for a year. When he returned he established a new home in Wisconsin that he shared with his lover, Mamah Borthwick Cheney, a former client. Like the hill towns he admired in Tuscany, his new complex would be a hilltop refuge, complete with a tower.

Initially referred to as a cottage for his mother, Taliesin I was constructed on thirty-one acres adjoining his sister Jane Porter's property in Spring Green in Wright's beloved Wisconsin River valley, where his ancestors had settled. His house, built of plaster, wood, and stone from a nearby quarry, was called Taliesin after a Welsh poet whose name meant "shining brow." Wrapping around the crest and into the slope of a large hill near his grandfather's homestead, it marked a return to the landscape that he had learned to love as a boy.

The driveway curled around the house, passing through stone piers between the hill and the residence. With its sculptures, pool, terraces, and stone walls, the garden was an integral continuation of the building's design. The entry was hidden within a sheltered stone loggia, establishing an intimate welcome. Perpendicular to the residential wing, which included a master bedroom suite, a guest room, two bathrooms, the kitchen, and the living-dining room, was the long drafting studio. Beyond and perpendicular to that was the farm unit, with its anchoring tower. Each zone of the U-shaped complex was connected to the others by open terraces or courtyards. Wright hoped to make Taliesin self-sustaining as a farm, a home, and an architectural studio, integrating and unifying all aspects of his life.

Inside the residential wing and studio, huge stone fireplaces served as the focal points of the main rooms, while panoramic views of the valley through ribbons of casement windows energized the spaces. Wright had taken elements of his Prairie Style concepts, enriched them with his European experiences, and produced an intimate and imaginative retreat that reflected his new-found freedom—his first natural house.

One afternoon in August 1914 Wright's new life suffered a terrible setback when a crazed houseman served lunch and then set fire to the house, murdering seven people with an axe as they tried to flee. Wright, working in Chicago at Midway Gardens, was called home to find Mamah Cheney, her two children, and four employees dead and his home partially destroyed. As he wrote in *Liberty* magazine in 1929, "In 30 minutes it had burned to the stonework or to the ground. The living half of Taliesin violently swept down in a madman's nightmare of flame and murder."

Highway 23
at County Road C
Spring Green,
Wisconsin

Designed in 1911
Partially burned in 1914

TALIESIN II

Ever resilient, Wright immediately rebuilt his house after the 1914 fire and tried to put his life back together. Although only the residential portion had been destroyed, Wright used the opportunity to make alterations to all parts of the complex, enlarging and adapting them to suit his expanding vision. The new house fell short of his ideal plans, but such was the reality of the ever-evolving Taliesin.

The rebuilding of Taliesin I to create Taliesin II was undertaken using the same materials—limestone, plaster, and wood—but the execution was more refined and less rustic than the earlier version. The masonry masses that survived were reworked so that the fireplaces received new mantel stones. Elevations became more complex. The rooflines of the living room and the studio were changed. In place of its pitched ceilings, the living room gained a recessed panel and the drafting room a shed roof with a reverse pitch section over the fireplace, which partially concealed a pocket art glass window.

The building and refurnishing of Taliesin II coincided with a period when Wright traveled frequently to Japan during construction of the Imperial Hotel, so the house was filled with his new art collections. Between 1917 and 1922 he brought home not only Japanese prints but also Japanese screens, textiles, metalwork, and sculptures and Chinese ceramics. Many pieces were built into the structure or strategically placed as integral parts of the architecture. The richness of the interiors was a result of the combination of these artworks and the simplicity of his own imaginative architecture.

But once again—eleven years later—fire destroyed Wright's home, again leaving his studio untouched. He described the event in *Liberty* magazine: "At twilight, the lightning of an approaching storm was playing. I came down from the little detached dining room on the hilltop to find smoke pouring from my bedroom. Again? There it was—Fire!"

Many people rushed to help, but the storm winds only made the fire worse. Miraculously, just as the fire reached the drafting room, the wind changed and blew it out. No lives were lost, but many valuable works of art were destroyed along with the house. Wright walked through the ruins, collecting fragments of the art, and then he wove these into Taliesin III, construction of which began immediately and formed the basis for the house that stands today.

22

Highway 23

at County Road C

Spring Green,

Wisconsin

Designed in 1914

Partially burned in 1925

IMPERIAL HoTEL ANNEX

Before Wright was contacted about creating plans for the luxurious Imperial Hotel (1915–23) in Tokyo (see pages 126–29), a simple frame building with forty-two guest rooms had been built next to the proposed hotel site. In 1919, just three months after work on the new Wright-designed hotel had begun, a fire broke out, entirely destroying the old wooden building in one and a half hours.

Because this auxiliary space was needed until the new structure could be completed, Wright was immediately called on to build a replacement. He designed a simple three-story, wooden building with a square central court and a connecting link to the new building. It was put up quickly and sparingly. Because Wright was allowed to live on site, using hotel services, he also created his own residence, a two-story apartment, in the new annex. During the next three years he and Miriam Noel, who would become his second wife in 1923, lived there during their extended stays in Tokyo.

Wright's quarters overlooked Japanese gardens below and consisted of a living room with a balcony, a bedroom, a dining room, and an upstairs studio in which he could also sleep. It was beautifully furnished with a grand piano, many Wright-designed wooden furnishings, and artwork he had collected. Notable were the innovative lighting fixtures that began as freestanding floor lamps and then joined the wooden arms projecting from the walls. Within the distinctive brick and stone fireplace a fire burned constantly. The carved wooden door at the entry was eventually moved to Taliesin to be used as its front door.

Beyond Wright's apartment, little is known of the annex. Reportedly it was on the verge of being condemned in 1922, when the north wing of the hotel was finished, but it was still needed for guests until the south wing could be completed. It was then abandoned. Amazingly, the annex withstood the great 1923 earthquake that undermined the hotel and the fires that followed, but it was weakened and no longer required. It presumably was demolished soon after.

Adjoining 1-1-1

Uchisaiwai-cho

Chiyoda-ku

Tokyo

Designed in 1919

Demolished in 1923

TALIESIN HYDRO HOUSE

Self-sufficiency was a goal at Taliesin. Wright, his family, and the apprentices raised their own food, had their own well and windmill, and supplemented the steam heat with fireplaces in most rooms. Taliesin relied on gas for lighting until 1920, when Wright decided to install his own hydroelectric power plant on the property.

Wright had reshaped and dammed the creek running through Taliesin to create a water garden at the base of the hill below his house. The hydroelectric plant, covered with a protective shelter, was placed on the lower dam. This turbine generated power for the house and pumped water up the hill to a reservoir. The pond water could not be used for drinking but was suitable for other purposes: feeding the pools and watering the gardens near the house and some tasks in the house.

Each morning, even on cold winter days, one of Wright's apprentices would rise at dawn, hike down the hill to start the turbine, hike back up, and fire up the wood stoves. Despite all the effort, the turbine was not powerful and was certainly undependable. The lights would often go dim, especially if a turtle, for instance, got caught in the mechanism. By the 1930s this power was supplemented with diesel-fed electric generators, which were used until the property received public power.

The shelter for the hydroelectric plant was built of boards and battens beneath a shingled roof. Its sloping rooflines and functional simplicity gave it the appearance of a Japanese temple sitting on a waterfall. The stone foundation was a part of the composition of retaining walls that worked their way from the dam and up the hillside to the house.

Years of struggle against the rushing waters eroded the structure, washing away one part after another. The remainder was removed during reconstruction of the upper and lower dams in 1946.

Taliesin

Highway 23 at County Road C

Spring Green, Wisconsin

Designed in 1920

Destroyed by 1946

OCATILLA

Responding to a request from Alexander Chandler to design a desert resort (see page 131), Wright gathered a fifteen-member entourage, left Wisconsin on a frigid January day in 1929, and headed for Chandler, an eponymous new community in central Arizona. Wright had met Dr. Chandler, a veterinarian-turned-development visionary, through his old friend and former apprentice Albert McArthur, who was building the Arizona Biltmore Hotel nearby (see page 130).

When they arrived, Wright's band of apprentices began to build a desert camp on Chandler's land to house themselves for the next five months. While others would come and go, the core group at Ocatilla, as the camp was called, consisted of George Kastner, Cy Jahnke, Henry Klumb, Vladamir Karfik, Don Walker, the William Weston family, Mrs. Taggertz (the cook), Wright, his wife, Olgivanna, and daughters Svetlana, twelve, and Iovanna, three.

Chandler Boulevard

at East 32nd Street

Phoenix

The camp structures consisted of simple board-and-batten boxes made of box board and covered with triangular white canvas roofs. The boards were painted a dusty rose like the desert sand, while the red triangles on the ends were the color of the ocotillo cactus flower. (Wright's misspellings of the word have resulted in the camp's being known variously as Ocatilla and Ocatillo.) The canvas-over-wood-frame wings of the roofs were hinged with rubber belting to open and close.

Designed in 1929

Partially burned in 1929

The fifteen camp buildings included sleeping boxes, a living room, a drafting room, a dining room, a kitchen, a garage, and an electrical plant. They rambled like a dotted, zigzag line around the natural flora, creating a central court for a campfire.

It was here that Wright fell in love with the desert light, especially when filtered through canvas. In his 1932 autobiography he wrote, "Since they will be temporary, call them ephemera. You will soon see them all like a group of giant butterflies—conforming to the crown of the outcropping of splintered rock gently rising from the desert floor."

With the Great Depression starting, financing for the Chandler hotel project was never secured, so Wright returned to Wisconsin in May. In July half of the camp burned. Wright tried to make arrangements to have it repaired, but because he never came back, what was left was abandoned. Its idea lived on, however, and became the prototype for Taliesin West eight years later.

HILLSIDE PLAYHOUSE I

When Wright established the Taliesin Fellowship in 1932, he remodeled his aunts' Hillside Home School II building for use as his own school. He had designed the building for them in 1902 near the original Hillside Home School (see pages 18–19), but it had been abandoned when the school closed in 1915. Wright converted the gymnasium wing into a theater, which would become the site of the third major fire to ravage Taliesin. Over the years this theater, which was called the playhouse, was modified many times and was used to entertain thousands of Taliesin guests.

The first remodeling, in 1933, created a small stage in a board-and-batten room. In later, gradual changes this space was expanded and the brightly colored, felt-appliquéd curtain reused by suspending it from ropes to fit the new, larger stage opening. The orchestra pit was outfitted with a sound system and a specially designed quartet stand. The seats were reset at a thirty-degree angle, which Wright called "reflex seating." One version had trays on the back of each chair to serve as a table for the person behind so that dinner could be served there. Each Saturday night the Fellowship would hold formal gatherings, usually featuring a concert by members of the group or a visiting artist. On other evenings movies, often foreign, were shown, and on Sundays the public was invited. Admission was fifty cents; coffee was served in red lacquered cups.

By 1950 the board-and-batten, multilevel interior had a balcony, which added to the dynamic interplay of projecting angles. A lounge area with a large fireplace occupied the rear of the room. Tall glass windows were covered with roller bamboo shades to control light. Custom-designed ceiling light fixtures were created using cubes and shelves projecting from a descending post like abstracted fruit and leaves growing from a branch. Reminiscent of a natural amphitheater in the woods, the space was filled with branches brought in from the outside and was both expansive and enveloping.

During the fall of 1952, leaf burning outside the playhouse went out of control and destroyed this wing of the school building. The adjoining dining room and the classrooms above also were lost. A Walt Whitman quotation on the wall to the right of the stage above the musicians burned but was reapplied to the wall of the new theater, which was built the next year. The space has continued to evolve in a Wrightian style and now has new seating and a different appliquéd curtain, an abstraction of the surrounding landscape.

Taliesin

Highway 23

at Hillside School Road

Spring Green,

Wisconsin

Designed in 1933

Burned in 1952

SHELTER-IN-THE-WASH

Rather than endure the discomforts of Wisconsin's coldest months, the Taliesin Fellowship established winter quarters in the Arizona desert. In the spring of 1937 Wright's entourage arrived at the base of the McDowell Mountains near the tiny community of Scottsdale and immediately began constructing a permanent camp while operating an architectural practice and school. The apprenticeship system of learning while doing was integral to the establishment and continued maintenance of what they called Taliesin West.

The first structure the apprentices built was a simple, multipurpose lean-to with a projecting roof. Made of box board, two-by-fours, and white canvas, the shelter was approximately forty feet long and open on one side. It represented yet another version of the tent construction Wright experimented with on the desert. The eleven distinctive poles extending from the framing gave it the appearance of a rectilinear tipi or a circus tent. On one end of this open-air headquarters a root cellar was built to store food. Adjoining it was the kitchen, which had only a two-burner stove, and a dining area with a simple table of wooden planks. John Howe, Wright's chief draftsman, set up his table at the other end; here he would translate Wright's vision for their desert home onto paper. A stone vault, the first permanent structure, was soon built nearby to house the studio's drawings.

Former apprentice Cornelia Brierly recalls that the young apprentices slept on the desert floor until they were given square white shepherds tents. Eventually some built their own box shelters to provide better protection from desert wildlife and weather. Various materials were tried for roofs, including sisal kraft paper and roofing paper, but canvas proved the most satisfactory. When the permanent Taliesin West structures were built within the year, the "shelter-in-the-wash" was no longer needed and was dismantled.

34

Taliesin West

Frank Lloyd Wright

Boulevard

Scottsdale, Arizona

(top right)

Designed in 1937

Demolished in 1938

SUN TRAP

The first permanent living quarters constructed at Taliesin West was the Sun Trap, a shelter built in 1937 for Wright, his wife, Olgivanna, and their twelve-year-old daughter, Iovanna. The massive corner fireplace and adjoining terrace wall were built of the rubble construction used throughout Taliesin West. Wood frames were built, filled with large desert rocks, flat side out, and filled in with a sandy concrete. The frames were then removed, leaving the stone fireplace wall in warm colors ranging from coral to rose to grayish purple. A concrete pad was poured for the floor, defining the dimensions of the shelter, which was partially enclosed with shiplapped redwood walls.

Instead of glass windows, adjustable white canvas side flaps and roof covers were used above the wooden walls. The center of the rooftop was stepped up in three layers with clerestory openings between them, permitting natural light into the core of the shelter. Sleeping boxes, one on each of three sides, were large enough for a thirty-inch-wide bed, a small closet, and a changing area. In one corner was a music "room," while in another an oleander bush screened a chemical toilet and a basin.

The front third of the structure, an open terrace with built-in seating, had a drafting table and Navajo rugs. It was a popular gathering place in the evenings, for a fire was always burning in the fireplace to cut the desert chill. These were primitive times at Taliesin West—living among rattlesnakes and other desert creatures, without plumbing systems and warmed only by fires. Somehow, the simplicity and rawness of life on the desert seemed to invigorate all who visited and lived there.

Once larger quarters were built for the Wrights, Sun Trap was used for guest or apprentice housing. In 1948 the building was disassembled. The foundation and fireplace became the basis for Iovanna's private quarters, the Sun Cottage, which still exists at Taliesin West.

35

Taliesin West

Frank Lloyd Wright

Boulevard

Scottsdale, Arizona

(bottom left)

Designed in 1937

Demolished in 1948

PLAZA HoTEL APARTMENT

The octogenarian Wright began spending more and more time in New York City in the mid-1950s. A major exhibition of his work, *Sixty Years of Living Architecture,* had just traveled around Europe and returned to a successful showing in its own pavilion (see pages 156–59) on the future site of the Guggenheim Museum. The architect had received several commissions in the region, and the complex negotiations for the Guggenheim (1943–59) were continuing.

Although construction of the museum did not begin until 1956, the planning process was all consuming. Wishing to be close to the project and have more space than a hotel suite could provide, in 1954 Wright established a temporary residence at his favorite hotel, the Plaza. During the next five years he and his wife, Olgivanna, spent considerable time in the three-room unit, which had once been the apartment of Diamond Jim Brady, the oversized celebrity and gambler. Wright used it as a combined residence and office, sometimes calling it Taliesin East. In this bustling center of activity the still-vigorous architect hosted many friends and prospective clients, including the actress Marilyn Monroe. (Wright's house design for her and Arthur Miller was never built.)

Wright was renowned for rearranging the furniture of any hotel room in which he stayed, but here he completely redecorated the suite. The palette—black, gold, plum, red, and peach—was unlike any he had previously used but seemed suited to this sophisticated city space. Unable to change the shape of the windows, he mounted round mirrors over their tops and installed lights behind them; long red velvet curtains hung from just below the ceiling. Gold Japanese paper was applied in wall panels. Some ready-made furniture was purchased, but Wright designed special tables, easels, and seats to be built by his apprentices; these were painted with black lacquer and edged in red. Peach-colored wool carpeting was installed throughout. As was his custom, Wright had a grand piano moved to the space and made a point always to have arrangements of fresh flowers and branches around.

The space remained as Wright had decorated it until it was demolished during a hotel remodeling.

Plaza Hotel

Fifth Avenue

at 59th Street

Suite 223

New York City

Designed in 1954

Demolished in 1968

HOUSES

The majority of Wright's work was residential, yielding 315 unique single-family houses. Only thirteen are completely gone and one partially demolished, a testament perhaps to their timeless appeal. Twelve of Wright's earliest commissions were remodelings of existing houses by other architects, only three of which are no longer here. The lost houses, three-fourths of which were built by 1920, fell to fires, a hurricane, and an earthquake as well as to urban blight, redevelopment, and neglect.

Wright's quest to create beautiful houses for American families dominated his career from beginning to end. He searched constantly for innovations in design and construction that would respond more effectively to the lifestyles, budgets, materials, technologies, and landscapes of Americans' informal and individualistic society.

Some clients were attracted to Wright's innovative ideas but perhaps thought that retaining him was too bold a step economically or stylistically. But he was quickly recognized as a masterful designer of the sort of interior details that could sensitively alter a Victorian structure's character and give it a fresh look. His early remodelings would cleverly open and energize spaces using wood banding, overhead light decks, spindled screens, and fret-sawn or solid-wood panels. His artistry was particularly visible in entries, stair halls, and dining rooms. Wright's straight lines, geometric forms, rich wood tones, and intimate scale replaced the fussy spaces of Victorian houses, creating the warmer, simplified feel encouraged by the magazines of the day.

The evolution of Wright's architectural philosophy is apparent in the range of his lost houses. In the Berry-MacHarg (1891) and Moore (1895) commissions, he experimented with traditional motifs, while the Harlan (1891) and Sullivan (1892) houses reflected Louis Sullivan's influence. With the Husser house (1899), he took an aggressive leap toward independence. The Prairie Style is represented by the Horner (1908), Steffens (1909), Angster (1911), and Little II (1912) (left) houses. Wright's Japanese years are marked by the Fukuhara house (1918) and his California period by the Barnsdall residence B (1920). The Pauson (1940) and Fuller (1951) houses exemplified early and late Usonian designs. Many of them were filled with specially designed decorative arts, much now also lost.

BERRY-MACHARG HOUSE

For a few of Wright's commissions, particularly those done from 1891 to 1893, when he worked for Louis Sullivan, the blending of his design skills with those of Sullivan has created some problems of clear attribution. Sullivan's influence on Wright is certain, but Wright brought his own artistry to their collaborations and greatly influenced the designs. In addition, the Berry-MacHarg design presents an unusual client attribution dilemma.

The MacHarg house that Wright spoke of designing appears to be the same as the Adler and Sullivan commission for C. H. Berry announced in the *Economist* in October 1891. It is believed to have been one of several residential commissions assigned to Wright, the firm's talented young apprentice. The only wood-frame structure the firm had ever designed, it cost $10,000.

Chicago directories list both Dr. Berry and William MacHarg at this address in 1893. MacHarg, a city sewerage engineer and plumbing contractor, worked closely with Adler and Sullivan and was well known to Wright, which may have been the reason he remembered the commission as his. (MacHarg later joined William Winslow and Edward C. Waller, two other early Wright clients, to form the American Luxfer Prism Company, for which Wright also worked briefly in 1897.) When Berry died in 1902, MacHarg purchased the house, retaining Sullivan to design a small remodeling in 1903.

The design owes a debt also to the Shingle Style houses of Wright's previous employer, Joseph Lyman Silsbee. A steep, shingled roof with dormers, many large casement windows, and an arched entry were characteristic of this popular style. Wright's interpretation combines these features with narrow clapboard below and plaster above a continuous band that connects the upper-story windows. Only the foundation of the 35-by-57-foot house is Roman brick. Wright's extensive use of simply turned spindled balustrades, similar to those on the balcony of his own children's playroom (1895) in Oak Park and in several other projects during the 1890s, provides a screen—a gentle guide—to those entering the house. Most houses of the time were entered directly through a center door, but here Wright was developing his favored technique of a more mysterious entrance. Despite the peaked roof, the house has a comfortable, well-proportioned horizontality. Unfortunately, little is known of its floor plan.

Located on a short street on Chicago's North Side, not far from Lake Michigan, the house was in an area becoming more densely populated. During the 1920s houses here were rapidly converted into apartments. The Berry-MacHarg residence was demolished in 1926, and an apartment building rose in its place.

40

4632 (formerly 3227)

Beacon Avenue

Chicago

(top right)

Designed in 1891

Demolished in 1926

HARLAN HOUSE

While working for Adler and Sullivan in 1888–93, Wright accepted commissions for seven private houses, which he designed after hours—a violation of his employment contract. Despite his efforts to conceal these "bootleg" jobs by using the name of his architect friend Cecil Corwin to announce the commissions in the trade press, he was eventually discovered by Sullivan. This house for Allison Harlan, designed in 1891 and built in Sullivan's neighborhood in 1892, led to Wright's departure from the side of his greatest teacher.

During his years with Sullivan, Wright had become skilled in the geometric, nature-based ornament the master preferred and used it here in fret-sawn panels across the front of the house. The conventionalized tracery patterns on the balcony and in the entry hall were similar to the motifs Wright used on the balcony and stairhall in the Charnley house in Chicago, done the same year for a Sullivan client. This, combined with the design's geometric freshness, could easily have given away Wright's authorship. In 1956 Wright told Dr. Harlan's daughter that it was the "first house built my own way."

Wright included other features that he developed further in his later Prairie Style houses. The low, hipped roof and broad, sheltering eaves, the indirect entrance and generous verandas, the casement windows, the spindled screens in the stairhall, and the simple geometric forms—all were unusual for the time and marked Wright's determination to break away from convention. The two-story house had six bedrooms, several of which opened onto balconies.

Dr. Harlan, a dentist, demanded several changes to Wright's plan. The fireplace was moved from the central hall into the open living room, which was then divided into two parts. In about 1904 Harlan traded houses with his neighbors, the Byrneses, who sold Wright's structure in 1912. Vacant for years, it became a neighborhood hangout. For a short time it was used as a nursing home and then fell into ruin. A fire caused enough damage to require its demolition.

4414 Greenwood Avenue

Chicago

(bottom left)

Designed in 1891

Burned in 1963

SULLIVAN HOUSE

Louis Sullivan's brother, Albert, commissioned him to design this townhouse for their mother, Adrienne. She died before it was completed, but Louis moved in and lived here until 1896, when he and his brother quarreled and he was forced to move out.

Because Sullivan was busy with commercial commissions, Wright was deeply involved in the design, although it was certainly a collaboration. The richly ornamented facade, for instance, was at least partly Sullivan's design. The carved limestone tympanum above the door as well as the cove molding and lion's head in the bedroom matched his designs for features in the Transportation Building at the World's Columbian Exposition of 1893, then being constructed. Simpler geometric patterns found in the glass and the decorative metalwork on the facade, more conventionalized and less sinuous than Sullivan's work, appear to be from Wright's hand. The crisp definitions of contrasting planes were sculptural—the second-story bay window projecting, the entry and first floor window receding. The elegant interior had elaborate mahogany paneling, arched hallways, and a mosaic floor in the entry hall.

The house continued as a private residence until the 1950s. After first being remodeled into apartments, it was converted into a neighborhood community center. Damage from an earlier fire and a leaky roof was compounded by extensive vandalism. By 1963 the elaborate sheet copper cladding the upper window bay and cornice, the art glass windows, the wrought-iron front door panel, and other decorative elements were gone, and the house was a ruin. Before it was demolished, the photographer Richard Nickel persuaded Southern Illinois University to save the once-elegant limestone facade, which he and his brother dismantled so that this work of art would not be lost forever. These building parts remain in the university's collection in Carbondale.

4575 Lake Avenue

Chicago

Designed in 1892

Demolished in 1970

43

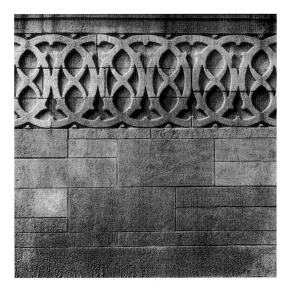

BASSETT HOUSE REMODELING

Wright left Louis Sullivan's office in early 1893 and established his own practice in the Schiller Building in downtown Chicago. One of his early independent commissions was this remodeling of an existing house into a combined office and residence for Howard W. Bassett, a homeopathic doctor. Wright redesigned the front part of the ground floor, converting the parlor and porch into a waiting room and examining room but leaving the other spaces as they were. Along with other exterior changes, a new sheltered entrance was added to provide easy commercial access while maintaining a comfortable, homey appeal.

125 South Oak Park

Avenue

Oak Park, Illinois

Designed in 1894

Demolished in 1922

This simple commission illustrates several of Wright's favorite techniques at the time, many of which he used in his own house (1889–98) on Forest Avenue in Oak Park. Polygonal bays created interest and relieved the boxiness of the space. The porch balustrades used the same spindles as those on the Berry-MacHarg house (1891) (see page 140) and on the playroom balcony (1895) in Wright's house. Diamond-paned glass on the ground floor resembled the windows in his own house, but the simple circular patterns in the upper windows were similar to those used in the Sullivan house (1892) (see pages 42–43). The exterior was covered with a wide shingle-and-batten band sandwiched between bands of plaster, producing a unique wall treatment that served to elongate the square facade. Wright never used this treatment again.

Dr. Bassett left Oak Park in 1900, but another physician, Leslie Beebe, occupied the space until 1921, probably leaving it intact. In 1922 all structures on the west side of Oak Park Avenue from Pleasant Street to South Boulevard, including the Bassett house, were demolished for development of the G. H. Schneider Building, which still houses many stores and offices.

MOORE HOUSE I
AND PERGoLA

329 Forest Avenue

Oak Park, Illinois

House designed in 1895;

mostly burned in 1922

Pergola designed in

1905; final portions

demolished by 1965

The prosperous attorney Nathan Grier Moore and his wife, Anna, owned several pieces of adjoining property down the street from Wright's Oak Park house. They first asked Wright to remodel an existing house but decided instead to move it, demolish yet another old house on the property, and build a new home there.

The Moores dreamed of a Tudor-style house, and although Wright at first resisted, in 1895 he designed for them an "Elizabethan" half-timbered house with only a few interpretive deviations. Placed on the far northern boundary of the property, it opened onto a large garden area to the south. Generous ribbons of windows welcomed sunlight and permitted wonderful views, yet its dark paneling and eight unique fireplaces gave it a clublike appeal. With this picturesque English country house in an American suburb, Wright demonstrated that he could do a masterful job of designing pattern-book houses.

Six years later Wright was asked to remodel another old house on the site for the Moores' daughter, Mary Hills, and her husband, Edward. Rejecting historic styles, Wright employed a Prairie Style design that completely concealed the old structure. This house was devastated by a fire in 1976 but was accurately rebuilt and stands in excellent condition today.

In 1905 the Moores asked Wright to design a pergola and garden pavilion for the garden between the two houses. A geometric design of trellis and brick piers ingeniously unified the two vastly different residences. Parts of this were torn down when a garage and greenhouses were added to the complex, but a section of it, in the southwest corner, remained until 1965.

The greatest loss to the property was caused by an early morning electrical fire in late 1922, which destroyed the entire top half of the grand Moore house. The Moores called on Wright again, this time to rebuild their house. The result eliminated the third floor; but while respecting the Tudor roots of the house, this was a bolder design, more Mayan than English. Only the ends of the house retained some half-timbering. The rich, integral ornament and exotic sculptural forms recall Midway Gardens (1913) (see pages 122–25) and the Imperial Hotel (1915–23) (see pages 126–29), completed during this period of Wright's career. This remodeled house remains an Oak Park landmark.

WALLER HOUSE REMODELING

At the turn of the century, Edward C. Waller, a pioneer real estate developer, was a commanding force in the Chicago area. He became a good friend of Wright's, providing the link to at least fifteen commissions, including several apartment complexes, resorts, his own vacation house, a bathing club, the Rookery Building remodeling, residential developments, the Roloson rowhouses, and Midway Gardens (see pages 122–25). Some of the most revolutionary were never executed.

The Wallers owned a twenty-four-room Victorian mansion on a beautiful wooded, six-acre parcel at a bend in the Des Plaines River. Wright's innovative Winslow house (1894) is still across the street. Like the Wrights, the Wallers were very social and loved parties, so an important part of Wright's remodeling of their residence was an octagonal party pavilion with a glass passageway that joined it to the house.

The remodeling also involved extending the dining room and adding a new kitchen and pantry wing, with bedrooms above. A built-in seat was placed beneath the 12½-by-6-foot dining room window, making the view of the woods and the river beyond a part of the room's design. Burlap was used as a wall covering above built-in cabinets, and oak panel moldings linked the openings and cabinetry. A new dining table and chairs, among Wright's earliest furniture designs, were created for the space. Wright also created a library table. Ample wood trim was added throughout but was particularly striking in the entry hall. Circular motifs in the stairhall balustrade were accentuated by a round copper urn Wright designed to sit on the newel post.

Waller lived here until his death in 1931 at age eighty-five. By 1939 the house was in poor condition, the river had become foul with pollution, and the site had lost its charm. The house was demolished that year.

Auvergne Place

near Lake Street

River Forest, Illinois

Designed in 1899

Demolished in 1939

49

WALLER STABLES, PoULTRY HOUSE, AND GATES

Auvergne Place

near Lake Street

River Forest, Illinois

Designed in 1901

Stables demolished in

1970s; poultry house

demolished in 1939

In 1901, two years after the Chicago real estate baron Edward C. Waller had Wright extensively remodel his grand Victorian mansion in River Forest, Illinois (see pages 49–50), he commissioned farm outbuildings for the estate, followed later by entry gates.

The gates marked the entrance to both his property and the Winslow house (1894) (opposite), designed by Wright on land carved from Waller's parcel. Winslow Brothers Ironworks, famous for executing the rich, flowing designs of Louis Sullivan, created Wright's modular, rhythmic design of straight lines and squares for the fence and gates. The swinging carriage gate was lost many years ago, and a 1986 street widening threatened to take the remaining fence. Fortunately, local preservation efforts prevailed. The stone pylons and iron panels remain, and the light fixtures have been reproduced.

Among the farm buildings was the poultry house, an airy structure that included a large roosting area, a special incubation and brooding room for the baby chicks, and generous glass and screen panels that terminated in large stone pylons topped with flower urns. Rising from the hipped roof were eight-foot-tall copper pylons, which served as vents.

Long, low stables housed the larger animals on the estate, as well as the carriages, hay, and ice. Wright topped them with triangular spiked vents similar to those he designed for his own Midway farm buildings at Taliesin in Wisconsin in the 1930s. An apartment on the second floor was for the coachman. Both floors had ample windows, giving the building a Prairie Style appearance. A drive bisected the two halves of the large shingle-covered structure, which was nestled in the wooded landscape between the house and the Des Plaines River.

After the home and poultry house were demolished in 1939, the stables were briefly used as a hostel. In 1947 the land was sold to a developer who built sixteen ranch houses on the old Waller estate. A large portion of the stables remained until the early 1970s, when they were demolished.

51

HUSSER HOUSE

The Husser house, the grandest commission Wright had yet received, took a dramatic, artistic step toward the open harmony of his Prairie Style houses. Rising from a narrow lot on the shore of Lake Michigan in Chicago's Buena Park neighborhood, it was designed for Helen and Joseph Husser and was built for $18,000. The contractor, William Adams, constructed four other Wright buildings, including one for himself the following year.

Built of yellow Roman brick, the house was trimmed with plaster, terra cotta, and stone and had a red tile roof. A notable Sullivanesque decorative frieze as well as arcades and massing enhanced the design. The cruciform plan was more dynamic than Wright's earlier work and created many fascinating spaces, each meticulously detailed. Expansive living quarters were placed on the second and third levels to take advantage of the views of the lake to the east and the city to the south. The entrance, hidden beneath the porte-cochère, opened to a stairhall, which led up to the dramatic spaces and views above. A large glazed, octagonal bay projected from the dining room, which had custom furniture complete with built-in light standards as part of the three-piece table. The fireplace was faced with a glistening glass mosaic in a wisteria design by Blanche Ostertag and crafted by Orlando Giannini. Another octagon, an open porch, extended from the living room.

By 1926 this area of the lake had been filled in to create more land for development. The Husser house then sat a half mile from the water, separated from it by a golf course and Lake Shore Drive. Eventually surrounded by apartments and commercial buildings, the house was dwarfed, its panoramic views and tranquil setting gone. This elegant house was demolished so that an apartment building could be built on the site.

730 (formerly 178)

West Buena Avenue

Chicago

Designed in 1899

Demolished in 1926

HEBERT HOUSE REMODELING

Alfred W. Hebert, a dentist, singer, and music enthusiast, bought at least six rental properties in his Evanston neighborhood and remodeled them all into Prairie Style dwellings, which in 1902–12 was at the peak of its popularity in the Midwest. Wright assisted with this one, the first, and the architect Walter Burley Griffin, once a Wright employee, is thought to have helped with another. But for the other houses Hebert did most of his own redesigning and contracting.

This gabled frame house was at least eight years old when Hebert purchased it. Wright's remodeling connected to it a small L-shaped outbuilding at the rear of the narrow lot and added a bathroom, but most of the changes were made to the front of the house. That entire facade was altered when a single-story, glazed conservatory with stucco walls was added beneath long bands of windows. The remaining first-floor exterior was then wrapped with stucco as well, while the second floor remained clapboard. Inside, an open, simple, geometrically designed wooden partition marked the dining room entrance. The bay windows were filled in to the check rail of the double-hung windows, and built-in cabinets were fitted beneath. Bands of wood delineated the dropped ceiling.

1014 Hinman Avenue

Evanston, Illinois

Designed in 1902

Burned in 1959

Through the years the house remained a private residence. One cold January night in 1959, just after a new owner had begun a major renovation, a fire started by workers in a faulty chimney on the second floor spread, destroying most of that floor and injuring three firefighters. During the expanded reconstruction, a decision was made to remove all of Wright's surviving first-floor interior alterations. Although the house still stands and is in good condition, the modified footprint of the structure is all that remains of Wright's work.

EAST ELEVATION

SHAW HOUSE REMODELING

Wright designed a remodeling for the townhouse of the Canadian businessman C. Thaxter Shaw, but the ultimate outcome remains something of a mystery. Although Wright prepared many pages of drawings, including several color renderings, no written or photographic accounts have been located to document that the remodeling was actually done. Local building records were lost in a 1922 fire, but the strongest indication that the building was modified is the change in its footprint on city maps between 1906 and 1914. A large addition matching the shape of Wright's design appears on the rear of the house.

Wright had originally been asked to design a large country house for Shaw earlier in 1906, but the client decided to drastically alter his city house instead. The proposed facade changes added a bank of tall, narrow windows with dormers above and a new first-floor entrance flanked by Wright's signature low, flat urns. A large addition was to be made to the rear, and both the first and second floors were to be completely reconfigured and thoroughly outfitted with custom Wright-designed decorative arts.

New fireplaces, numerous art glass windows, and a wisteria-patterned glass mosaic like one at the Darwin Martin house (1904) in Buffalo, New York, were also to be installed. Wright's drawings show rectilinear Prairie Style dining furniture and light fixtures similar to those created in 1906 for the Robie house in Chicago, plus many other cabinets and seating pieces. George Neidecken of Neidecken and Walbridge, a Milwaukee designer, prepared at least one of the renderings and would customarily have overseen the fabrication of the decorative arts for Wright during this period. Curiously, there are no records of any such activity in Neidecken's extensive archives.

Shaw, who was prominent in the leather business, lived in his house until his death in 1927. Another leather merchant and Wright client, Thomas Edward Wilder of Elmhurst, Illinois, may have linked Shaw with Wright. Shaw's house was demolished in 1971 so that a high-rise could be constructed on the site.

3466 (formerly 310)

Peel Street

Montreal

Designed in 1906

Demolished in 1971

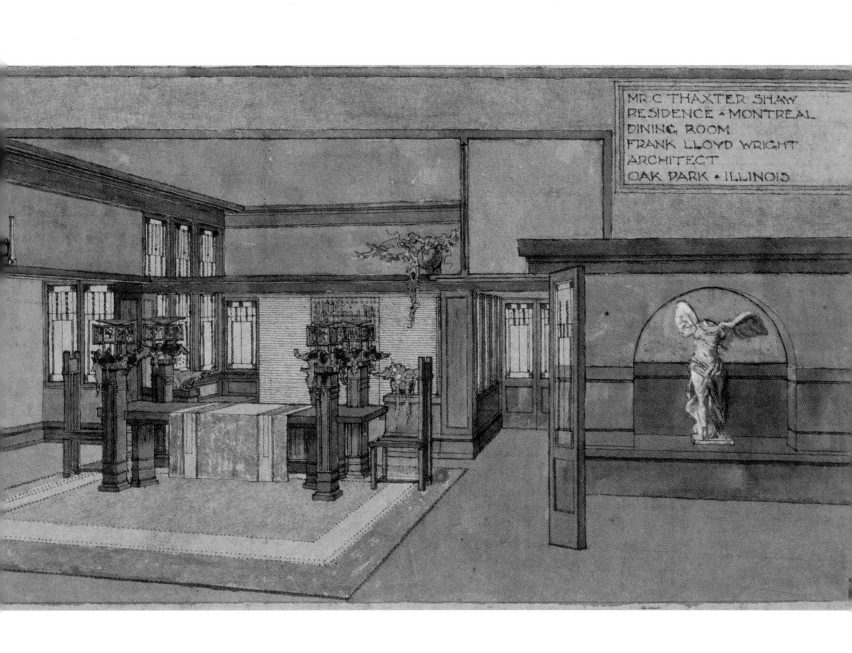

MR C THAXTER SHAW
RESIDENCE - MONTREAL
DINING ROOM
FRANK LLOYD WRIGHT
ARCHITECT
OAK PARK - ILLINOIS

HORNER HOUSE

This mature Prairie Style house in Chicago's Birchwood area, designed for Lena Kent Horner and her husband, Samuel, was stucco with wood trim. Long bands of windows and extended balconies increased the interior's spaciousness by reaching outside the confines of the walls. The design is similar to the Laura Gale house in Oak Park, which Wright designed in 1909 and whose owner was acquainted with the Horners.

Unlike the Gale house, the Horner residence had a shallow, hipped roof rather than a flat one. Its design was larger and more complex, yet it used cantilevers in a similar fashion. Its sharp-edged, cross-axial plan, delineated by bands of wood that defined the planes and masses of the well-balanced sculpture, was more like that of Wright's DeRhodes house (1906) in South Bend, Indiana. Broad entry stairs rose to spacious, open living and dining areas, both of which led to terraces. Upstairs, projecting balconies extended the house outward. Built-in cabinets, careful ceiling details, and wooden decks spanning the spaces added to the clean geometry.

The client connection for this house may have originated in two ways. Samuel Horner was president of the Horner Piano Company in Chicago, where Wright, a frequent piano buyer, could have been a customer. Lena Horner's brother, George Kent, was an Oak Park resident and realtor who served as manager of the Cook County Board of Realtors. He must have been well aware of Wright's popularity and certainly would have known Wright's clients Thomas and Laura Gale.

In 1926, eight years after her husband's death, Lena Horner, then the president of the company, moved the business and her residence to Evanston. The once-quiet Birchwood area became increasingly commercial, with more and more apartments replacing single-family houses. The house deteriorated and was eventually razed to make way for a two-story, four-unit townhouse.

1331 Sherwin Avenue

Chicago

Designed in 1908

Demolished in 1952

STEFFENS HOUSE

Another of Wright's Prairie Style houses in the Birchwood neighborhood was the Steffens house, and it too was eventually crowded out by apartments. An unusual Prairie design, it offered one of Wright's few one-and-a-half-story, balconied living rooms.

Resting on a ridge close to Lake Michigan, the house was opened to panoramic views through rows of clear art glass windows. They were flecked with touches of blue and yellow that appeared to be abstractions of the sun and waves beyond. Spindled screens partially concealed spaces, adding drama to the entrance. Tall windows in the front bay stopped short of the roofline. A layer of clerestory windows was set above them but was recessed beneath the eaves, leaving outside balconies on either side. Although the shallow, hipped roofs, central fireplace, wide overhangs, and indirect entrance were typical Wright techniques, the floor plan was unique. Flanking the grand living space was the dining room in one direction and an open porch in the other. Behind the fireplace the service area was recessed a half story so that the second-floor bedrooms above could have a full story beneath the roof.

Built for Oscar Steffens, a banker, the house was sold within two years to Otto Bach, whose brother, Emil, would become a Wright client three years later, building just three blocks away.

Located on a busy intersection and surrounded by commercial buildings, the Steffens house suffered for thirty years. In the 1930s it was converted into a restaurant. Its cream-colored stucco walls were eventually covered with gray asphalt shingles, and the wood trim was painted red. Most of the trees and shrubbery on this once-idyllic site were removed so that the grounds could be paved for parking. Finally, in 1963, the building was demolished. Today an apartment building stands in its place.

7631 Sheridan Road

Chicago

Designed in 1909

Demolished in 1963

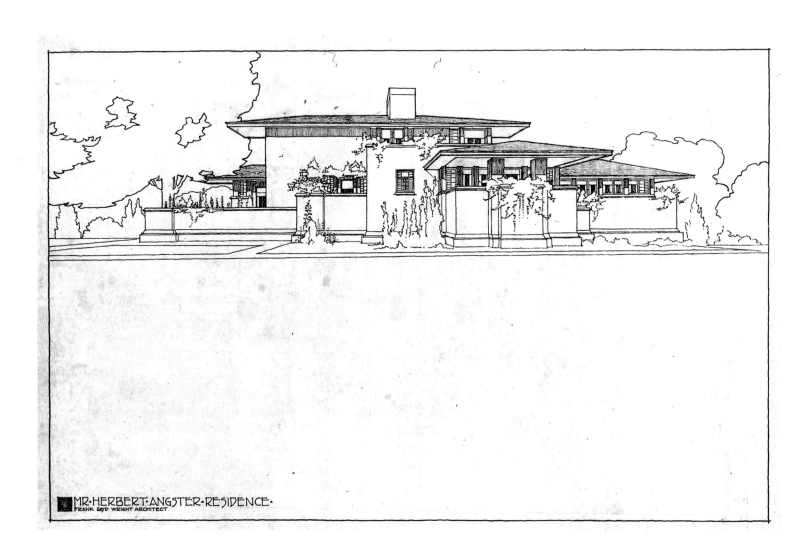

MR·HERBERT·ANGSTER·RESIDENCE·
FRANK LLOYD WRIGHT ARCHITECT

ANGSTER HOUSE

605 Bluff (formerly

Blodgett) Road

Lake Bluff, Illinois

Designed in 1911

Burned in 1956

The Angster house was designed just after Wright returned from his sojourn in Europe. Designed at Taliesin (1911–59), his new residence in Spring Green, Wisconsin, it shared some of that building's rustic simplicity and sense of seclusion. The house was graceful in its straightforward functionality and its simple, open plan. Its Prairie Style grammar is cleaner, the lines are crisper, and the spaces more flexible than in Wright's earlier Prairie houses.

Dramatically sited on a precipitous bluff overlooking Lake Michigan, this design sought to take full advantage of the view and the breezes. On the street side, however, it was nearly concealed by landscaping, giving it maximum privacy. A large terrace had trellises and removable screens and was eventually glassed in because it was often used for dining (there was no other dining space). Herbert, a plumbing manufacturer, and Blanche Angster had no children, so there was just one bedroom suite with its own terrace on the main floor. Guest and servants rooms were upstairs.

Blanche Angster was a younger sister of the attorney and Wright patron Sherman Booth, whose extensive Wright-designed residential development in Glencoe, Illinois, also began construction in 1911. She was also the long-time executive secretary of Anita McCormick Blaine, a well-known Chicago philanthropist. Blaine's father, Cyrus McCormick, was a Sullivan client, and her brother, Harold McCormick, in 1907 had commissioned Wright to design a house, which was never built.

The Angsters were divorced in the 1920s, but Blanche continued to live in the house. As the years passed she became more and more reclusive, fencing the property and allowing it to deteriorate and trash to accumulate. Enjoying the privacy of the surrounding woods, she continued to live in the house for thirty years, until it was destroyed by fire in 1956. The remains were bulldozed over the bluff to the lake, and the street was later renamed and redeveloped with several new houses.

LITTLE HOUSE II

Northome, the second house that Wright designed for Mary and Francis Little, was much grander than the Littles' earlier home (1903) in Peoria, Illinois, because it was also intended to serve as a private concert hall for Mary Little. Stretching across a knoll overlooking Lake Minnetonka in the countryside near Minneapolis, it was surrounded by woods. The enormous living room, more than fifty feet long with its own grand entrance and grand piano, became a quiet shelter in nature, a suitable partner for the sounds of music. A large open terrace connected it to a freestanding screened pavilion, providing further opportunities for enjoying this lyrical site.

The living room ceiling appeared to float above two layers of delicate art glass windows, their tiny triangular panes glistening like the water in the lake. Overhead, an art glass skylight released the airy space even further. Elaborate oak bands and decks wrapped and defined the spaces, accentuating the linear quality of the house. The remainder of the plan was also unusual: the dining, kitchen, and service areas were one floor below in the attached wing, with the family's bedrooms above them. As for the interior furnishings, some Wright-designed pieces of furniture were brought from their previous house, while others he newly designed.

The Littles were prosperous, educated, loyal, and patient, waiting six years for Wright to complete their country house. They stood by him when he was pursued by creditors and the law and even provided his family emergency refuge at one point. In 1972, however, the Little descendants chose to build a new house on the site, but local zoning permitted only one. Alerted to the impending demolition of the Wright house, the Metropolitan Museum of Art arranged to document it and salvage what it could. The living room was reinstalled in the American Wing of the museum, and other rooms were sold to museums in Allentown, Pennsylvania (see pages 64–65), and Minneapolis.

Rural Route 3

Wayzata, Minnesota

Designed in 1912

Demolished in 1972

FUKUHARA HOUSE

While supervising construction of the Imperial Hotel (1915–23) in Tokyo, Wright was asked to design at least seven houses, another hotel, a theater, and a school. One of the three houses actually constructed, the Fukuhara house was the country retreat of Arinobu Fukuhara, the founder of the Shiseido Company, a cosmetic manufacturer. It was commissioned by his son, Shinzo, who established the Japan Amateur Photographers Association.

To lose a building with such a unique setting and floor plan is particularly tragic. Located southwest of Tokyo near Gora, the house sat high on a rock cliff in the mountainous area on the eastern slope of Mount Soun. This wooded resort area was popular with foreigners because of the abundance of mineral springs and spectacular views. Wright's mother visited the house, which was not completed until 1920, while it was still under construction.

Built of wood with a heavy tile roof, the house had a square central courtyard, glassed in on all sides, with a pool fed by a hot mineral spring. Beneath the low, hipped roofs, plaster walls rose from a rugged stone base, similar to the rock formations on the site. The two-story living room featured a massive stone fireplace and dining area with a balcony above. Guest rooms were in one direction off the atrium, while the family's private quarters were in a semidetached pavilion in the other direction. The house appears related to both Wright's Hollyhock house (1917) in Hollywood and his Wisconsin home, Taliesin II (1914). All share zoned floor plans and an inward orientation, but the Fukuhara house is the only one with a completely enclosed central court.

67

During the destructive Kanto earthquake of 1923, which was more devastating in the Kangawa prefecture than in Tokyo, the house was completely destroyed and the owner injured. The living room section tumbled thousands of feet down the cliff. Because it was located on a remote site and stood only briefly and because few photographs of it have been found, the Fukuhara house remains one of Wright's more mysterious buildings.

Hakone, Japan

Designed in 1918

Destroyed by

earthquake in 1923

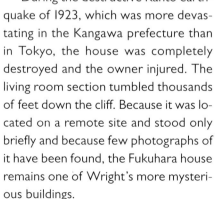

BARNSDALL RESIDENCE B

For eight years, from 1916 to 1924, Wright worked with the oil heiress and theater producer Aline Barnsdall to create a planned arts community on Olive Hill in Hollywood overlooking Los Angeles. It included cultural, commercial, and residential components with elaborate gardens and watercourses. Hollyhock house, her own home, was the first structure to be built in 1917. Residence B was one of the few others completed. At different times both Barnsdall and Wright lived here.

Because Wright was absorbed in his work in Japan, his apprentice Rudolph Schindler did the drawings for the original residence B, a three-story, plaster-and-wood structure built on the west side of a steep hill on Edgemont Avenue. Much simpler in design than Hollyhock house, it nonetheless shared its wood-frame and hollow-tile construction. It had a large two-story living space with a balcony and skylight and one-story alcoves on either side of the central space that were used as the library and dining areas. On the third level were three bedrooms, two and a half bathrooms, and a covered sleeping porch.

Barnsdall used the house intermittently. In 1923 Wright rented it for four months and did some remodeling—enclosing the sleeping porches, adding bedrooms and bathrooms, putting a second story over the garage, and making numerous changes to the exterior. His corbeled posts beneath the balcony and at the entrance drive were decorated with colorful geometric stencils, which also ornamented some of the lapped boards he wrapped around the balcony. Proposed ground-floor alterations for his studio were never completed.

Four years later Barnsdall donated her home, Hollyhock house, to the City of Los Angeles, retaining ownership of residence B. In 1928 she hired Schindler to remodel it again, creating a second-story bedroom suite over the garage and expanding on Wright's decorative details. She resided in the house whenever she was in Los Angeles and died here in 1946. It was still owned by the family but had decayed considerably when it was condemned and demolished eight years later.

1645 Vermont Avenue

Hollywood, California

Designed in 1920

Demolished in 1954

PAUSON HOUSE

The Pauson house was an artistic, meticulously crafted example of the pre-formed, desert rubble-wall construction that Wright had introduced three years earlier in his nearby winter home in Scottsdale, Taliesin West (1937–59). The Pauson sisters, Rose and Gertrude, potters and weavers from San Francisco, were well known for their personal style and sophisticated tastes. Frequent guests at the Arizona Biltmore Hotel (see page 130), they found a site close by and commissioned a vacation retreat. It would stand for less than two years, although its masonry chimney still remains a half century later.

This ruin captures the primitive, pre-Columbian feeling of the original structure. Walls of lapped wood over canted, dark red stone and concrete rose from the desert floor like an excavated temple. This austerity suited the site. Inside, the house was constructed as if it were a fine piece of furniture, each board custom milled six times before being carefully finished. The two-story living room had twelve-foot-high windows opening to outdoor terraces that served to double the living space and embrace the landscape beyond. Typical of Wright's Usonian houses, the open side of the house was opposite a closed, private side, with massive stone walls providing protection from desert winds and intense heat. The long, narrow plan placed the bedrooms on the upper level with a balcony overlooking the living-dining spaces, while the kitchen and servants rooms were on the lower level with the grand living area.

A tenant was staying in the house when it caught fire on a cold evening

in 1942. It is believed that sparks from the fireplace ignited the handwoven curtains nearby. The house quickly burned to the ground, leaving only the massive stone chimney. The ruin became a popular local landmark of sorts. When the site was eventually needed for a road in 1979, the ruin was moved and now rests at the entrance to a subdivision.

Orange Road

Phoenix

Designed in 1940

Burned in 1942

FULLER HOUSE

Mr. and Mrs. Welbie L. Fuller, who lived in Michigan, built their vacation house on a beautiful wooded site in Mississippi, just seventy feet from the Bay of St. Louis. Knowing that tidal waves could pose problems, Wright took special precautions with the house. The building system used poured concrete and steel columns to anchor the solidly built structure. Extending from the concrete block core was a grid of four-by-four posts, which were filled in with wallboard to create room partitions.

The living areas were raised to the second and third levels, nestling the house within the longleaf yellow pines like a tree house. Vertical elements of the long glass windows and doors mirrored the vertical rhythm of the surrounding pine trees, relating the building to its site. Yet the design was decidedly horizontal, with a solid utilitarian directness. Facing southwest, the spacious residence was 114 feet long and had a 30-foot-long sun deck connecting it to a guest house.

The Fuller house was one of Wright's Usonian houses, which he based on principles developed to reduce costs and simplify design. Like all the Usonians, it was constructed on a modular system, here a square grid. The Usonian format also called for standardized natural materials, flat roofs, zoned plans, and a large living space that opened to views of nature. The Fuller house was fully outfitted with custom furniture, both built-in and freestanding. Leonard Spangenberg, the supervising apprentice, reported that only the finest materials and craftsmanship were used. Unlike other Usonians, which had concrete floors throughout, the Fuller house had wood floors on all but the ground level, where a concrete pad was poured. The color scheme of soft gray and rich brown was drawn from the colors of pine tree bark.

The house survived Hurricane Betsy in 1965 with no structural damage. Despite all preventive strategies, however, it succumbed to the giant tidal wave brought by Hurricane Camille four years later. The house was completely swept away, including even Wright's original presentation drawing, which was hanging on the wall.

317 Sandy Hook Drive

Pass Christian,

Mississippi

Designed in 1951

Destroyed by

hurricane in 1969

Wright's interest in economical housing made him a clever designer of multiple dwellings as well as single-family houses. Of his more than one thousand designs, built and unbuilt, only twenty-one were for multiunit housing, and of these just eleven were constructed. Only the Roloson rowhouses (1894) in Chicago, four Richards duplexes (1916) in Milwaukee, and the Mallery quadruple house (1938) in Ardmore, Pennsylvania, remain, along with the surviving units of the Waller Apartments (1895) in Chicago.

Tragically all five of Wright's apartment buildings have been demolished in part or full. Three of them were designed in 1895, among them the Francis Apartments (right). These commissions led to another proposed multifamily building, the huge Lexington Terrace project for Chicago commissioned by Edward C. Waller Jr. This ambitious project remained on Wright's drafting tables from 1901 through 1909 but was never built. An extension of the 1895 Francisco Terrace concept, it encompassed more than two hundred units divided between two center-court buildings.

Many other apartment buildings were proposed by Wright over the years, but none was constructed. The eight-unit Belknap Apartments (1894) for Chicago, the Larkin workers rowhouses (1904) for Buffalo, New York, and the McArthur Apartments (1905) for Chicago offered few innovations but achieved Wright's objective of making small spaces feel larger. However, projects devised in the late 1920s and 1930s were some of Wright's most creative and ambitious work of the period. The Noble Apartments (1929) for Los Angeles, St. Mark's Tower (1929) for New York City, Grouped Towers (1930) for Chicago, and Crystal Heights (1939) for Washington, D.C.—high-rise structures to be built of reinforced concrete—all used a taproot-type design with cantilevered floors that freed outside walls for terraces, balconies, and generous glass walls. In 1952 Wright also designed a Pittsburgh apartment development based on a triangular module for Edgar Kaufmann, owner of the Wright-designed Fallingwater (1935).

Each of Wright's multiunit designs is yet another manifestation of his principles of organic architecture, his attempt to improve the quality of people's lives through architecture by opening spaces, respecting human scale, and devising construction efficiencies.

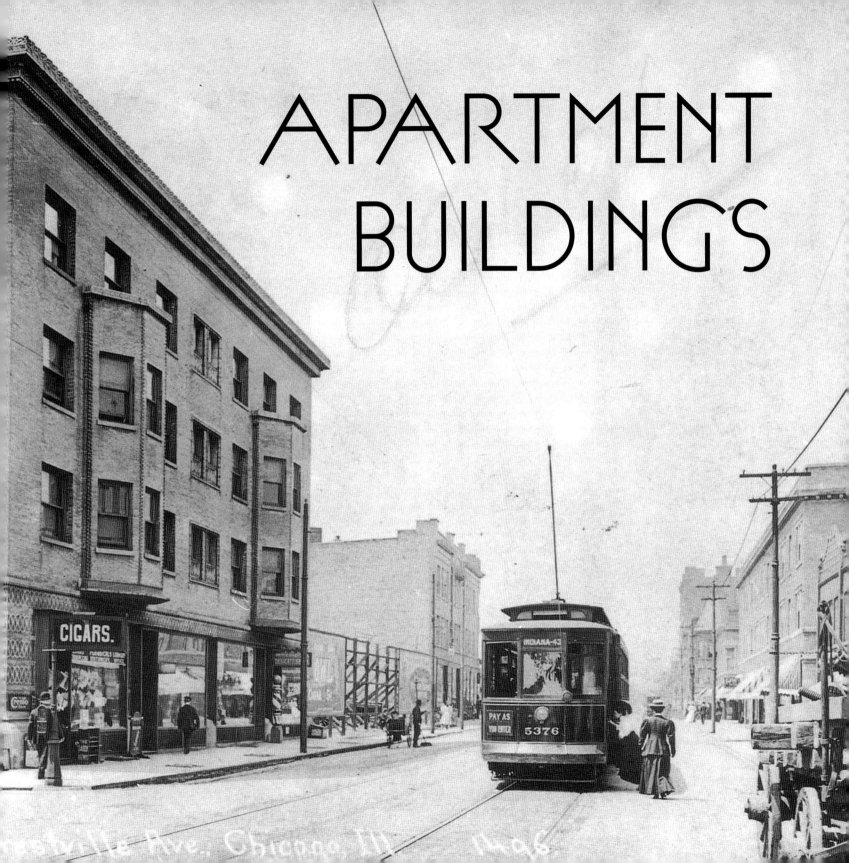

APARTMENT
BUILDINGS

FRANCIS APARTMENTS

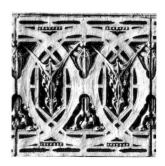

Wright's largest multiple dwelling, an elegantly simple one, was the U-shaped, four-story apartment building in Chicago that he designed for the Terre Haute Trust Company of Indiana. This richly surfaced, polychromatic structure contained many of the elements Wright used in other commissions of the time and reflected the teachings of his mentor, Louis Sullivan.

Here Wright successfully created a horizontal look despite the building's height by alternating bands of rich ornament with simple surfaces. Above the buff Bedford limestone base was a band of cream-colored terra cotta set in alternating rows with more stone. The remainder of the building was yellow brick. Its ornament, proportions, and massing all relate to Wright's Charnley house (1891) in Chicago and the Winslow house (1894) in River Forest, Illinois.

The prevailing circular motif, integral to the decorative composition, is more graphic and modular than in Sullivan's work. Wrought-iron gates, no doubt manufactured by Wright's friend and client William Winslow, captured the spirit of Sullivan's terra-cotta patterns, but each of Wright's designs draws on the innate characteristics of the respective materials for its power. The wrought iron was more linear, the terra cotta more plastic. Tiny beadwork and custom handling of the extremely long Roman bricks created more ornament on the building's facade, as did the decorated cornice, the last Wright used before abandoning that traditional architectural contrivance. The exaggerated stylobate, or base (see pages 74–75), established a strong connection with the earth and was a feature Wright favored in his early career.

76

The 43rd Street side of the ground floor was designed for shops with a mixture of one- to three-bedroom units behind them and on the three floors above. The entry was trimmed in marble and tile mosaic, and the bathrooms were tiled. Each unit had a fireplace and was detailed in white oak. The courtyard plan and large windows offered generous light to all units.

The building stood empty for about ten years before it was demolished in 1971. In the 1980s the property was redeveloped with a modern commercial building along 43rd Street.

4304 Forestville Avenue

Chicago

Designed in 1895

Demolished in 1971

FRANCISCo TERRACE
APARTMENTS

253–57 Francisco
Avenue

Chicago

Designed in 1895

Demolished in 1974

In 1895 Wright was asked to design two other apartment buildings, more modest units for working-class tenants. They were his first commissions from Edward C. Waller, who would become a loyal patron. Waller and Wright joined forces to find new ways of providing economical housing for Chicago's working poor.

Wright's utilitarian, central-courtyard design for Francisco Terrace encouraged a community feeling and permitted fresh air and a gardenlike setting, attributes that improved the desirability of the small quarters. He would continue to search for new solutions to satisfy the need for attractive, inexpensive housing, making units more open to a court, just as his Usonian houses forty years later were more open on their garden sides than on their front facades.

Francisco Terrace's appearance conveyed straightforward simplicity. The terra cotta of the arched entrance and stair towers provided the only ornamentation beyond the artful manipulation of the masonry itself. Each of the forty-five primarily two-bedroom apartments had its own outside entrance, with those on the second floor opening onto a wooden balcony with spindled balustrades. All were linked to the four corner stair towers, with their hipped roofs and open terra-cotta tracery. Despite their economical rent (an unusually low $12 per month for four small rooms, including steam heat), the apartments had an inherent sense of dignity and style. This homey feeling was particularly attractive to newlyweds, leading to the building's nickname, "Honeymoon Court."

As the years passed, larger families moved into the West Side apartments and maintenance became a problem. In 1974, after eighty years of hard use, the building was demolished. The entrance archway, with its Sullivanesque spandrels, was salvaged and incorporated into a new apartment building with a similar central-court design on Lake Street near Euclid Avenue in Oak Park, Illinois. The original site remains a vacant lot.

WALLER APARTMENT UNIT

At the Waller Apartments, the floor plans for most of the units, the rents, and the design efficiencies resembled those of Francisco Terrace (see pages 78–79), which practically adjoined them on the same block. This low-cost housing project, named for the developer Edward C. Waller, actually was designed first and appears to have been the prototype for the Francisco Terrace apartments.

To make the building affordable, Wright simplified the construction techniques, even setting studs sideways to reduce the size of the partitions, while Waller agreed to accept a return on his investment of only three percent instead of the customary six percent.

Symmetrical and modular for efficiency of construction, the apartments were simply constructed of a hard-fired yellow brick and Bedford limestone with little ornament. Some red terra cotta and simple beadwork at the cornice added to the subtle masonry delineation of the windows and doorways.

Each of the twenty units was rented for a bargain $12 per month to clerks, salespeople, and factory workers. All opened onto a rear porch, which was less than ten feet from the neighboring building. Four units were clustered together in each of five two-story sections, and these were separated from the others by a fire wall. The four-room units, which included no special features, contained a living room, a kitchen, and two bedrooms in less than five hundred square feet.

The building was converted into cooperative apartments in 1944 and had deteriorated significantly by 1968, when a fire destroyed most of the second unit from the west end. Efforts are now under way to stabilize the structure by first renovating one of the remaining apartment units as a model for rehabilitating the others. If successful, this venture may lead to reconstruction of the missing piece after three decades.

2852–54 West Walnut Street

Chicago

(top right)

Designed in 1895

Burned in 1968

MUNKWITZ DUPLEX APARTMENTS

The Munkwitz Apartments used standardized components that Wright and Arthur L. Richards developed as part of the American System-Built Houses. This innovative method, also known as Ready-Cut, relied on factory-made units and a uniform building process to cut labor costs at the building site.

Early in his career Wright became enamored of the machine, which he saw as an artist's tool to achieve efficiencies yet preserve style, and he expressed interest in modular housing. Richards, a Milwaukee real estate investor, developer, and promoter, shared this vision. He collaborated with Wright on a variety of Wisconsin projects from 1911 to 1917 and provided many contacts during this unsettled period in Wright's life.

The two apartment buildings, each with flats for four families, were built of precut parts assembled quickly on site. Similar to the six model houses and duplexes built for Richards the previous year on Burnham Street, which were variations of the Ready-Cut system, these two also drew on Prairie styling for their designs. Drawings for the two buildings, designed to be completed without Wright's presence, were done by Wright's draftsman Antonin Raymond, with oversight left in the capable hands of the architect Russell Barr Williamson, who continued to work with Richards after he left Wright's office in 1917.

The design, known as American Model J-521, resembled Wright's 1907 proposal for a "Fireproof House for $5,000," with its flat roofs, stucco walls delineated with wood banding, and ribbon windows; no other examples of this model were ever built. Each building was two stories high and had two double units connecting around a court. Their scaled-down, informal plan included a living room with a fireplace and a dining ell, a kitchen, a bathroom, and two bedrooms, which faced the rear. They reportedly cost only $20,000 to build.

Although Richards collaborated with Wright on the system design, another real estate investor, Arthur R. Munkwitz, owned these apartments. He and Richards were partners in the American Realty Service Company, which operated from the same office. The apartments were occupied until 1973, when the property was sold to the City of Milwaukee so that West Highland and 27th Streets could be widened. Despite the objections and testimony of many, the apartments were demolished the following year.

1102–12 North

27th Street

Milwaukee

(bottom left)

Designed in 1916

Demolished in 1974

To Frank Lloyd Wright no building—indeed, no part of a building—was unimportant. Claiming that he was as happy designing a chicken coop as a cathedral, he conscientiously applied to auxiliary projects such as outbuildings and annexes as much creativity and innovative problem solving as he gave to the primary buildings that are most remembered. While these service buildings were integral components of a larger commission, they were also individual structures with their own stories. Wright designed more than fifty of them, one for every ten of his principal buildings.

One-fifth of these secondary structures have been destroyed. Probably the greatest loss was the greenery-filled conservatory (1904) of the Darwin Martin house in Buffalo, New York (right), which spiraled into decay during the Great Depression and was razed in 1959. Although such structures could easily be dismissed as marginal works, all were part of the creative corpus of an architectural and artistic genius. Their significance lies not in their size but in this innovator's response to a particular problem. Some of the work forecasts later applications of design techniques, demonstrating how Wright's ideas evolved. As part of overall designs, they provide personal glimpses of clients' everyday lives and interests that may not be as visible in their houses alone. They also reflect the times, reminding us of the social, economic, and technological trends of the era: the shift from carriages to automobiles, the impact of railroads, patterns in leisure activities, the common use of servants, agricultural pursuits of the wealthy, and early-twentieth-century interest in garden design.

Unfortunately, because these buildings have often been treated as peripheral, they have not benefited from the photographic documentation or publication record of the primary structures. Little is known about most of those that have been demolished, and some in fact disappeared without a trace. While exterior photographs are rare, interior photographs are practically nonexistent.

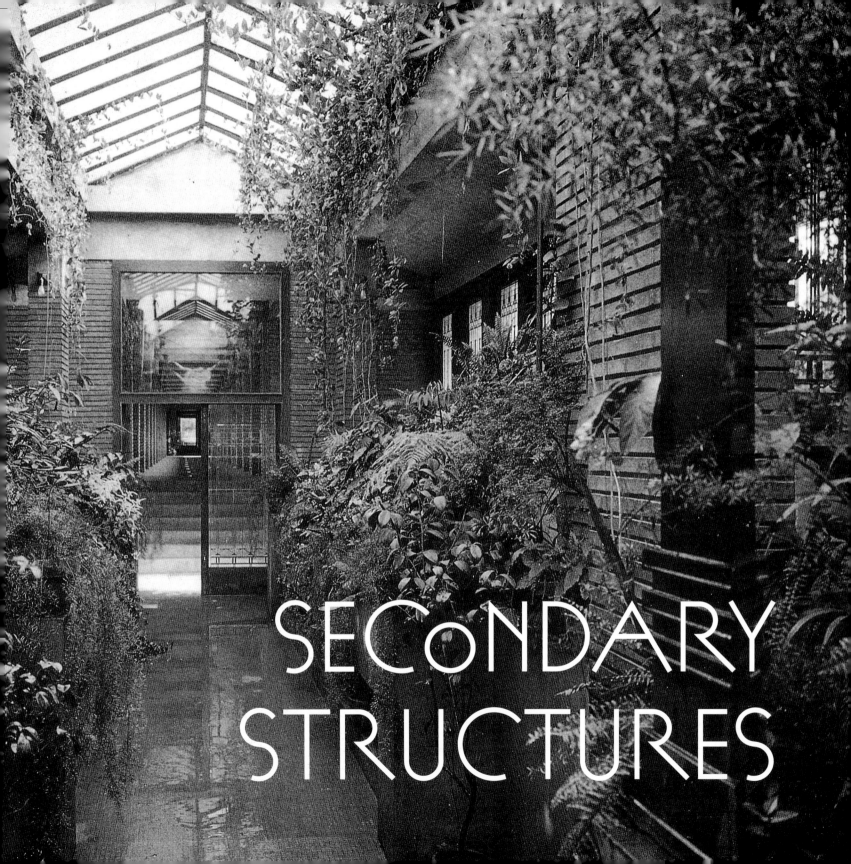

SECoNDARY
STRUCTURES

CHARNLEY STABLES

When his magnificent Auditorium Building in Chicago was finally completed in 1890, Louis Sullivan left on an extended vacation, taking the train first to California for a two-month visit and then on to New Orleans. There he met his friends Helen and James Charnley, who owned a Chicago lumber company and who the following year would commission him to design a house in Chicago. The Charnleys took Sullivan to Ocean Springs, a small rustic town on the eastern shore of Biloxi Bay, where he stayed for two weeks and regained his health. He was charmed by the wild forest surrounding the acreage they had purchased for a vacation home. There they asked him to design a beach house, a guesthouse, and stables. Sullivan also decided to build a vacation retreat for himself in Ocean Springs (see page 85).

While working for Adler and Sullivan from 1888 to 1893, Wright was often assigned to help with the few residential commissions the firm accepted. It is possible that Wright, back in Chicago, was asked to quickly draw the designs for both the Charnleys' and his *lieber Meister's* vacation house complexes and forward them to Mississippi so that Sullivan could turn them over to a local carpenter before returning north. But it is likely that Sullivan played a considerable role in the designs.

The Charnley stables, barely visible in the woods at the back of the property, had a steeply pitched roof, an octagonal tower, and a porch to take advantage of the ocean breezes. Little is known about the floor plan, but the structure included an apartment for servants as well as stalls for horses. The picturesque Shingle Style building with polygonal forms was executed with a geometric clarity that resembled Wright's own Oak Park house (1889–98) and prefigures his Emmond house in LaGrange, Illinois, and Parker house in Oak Park, both of which date from 1892 and have similar facade profiles.

So pleased were the Charnleys that the next year they commissioned Sullivan to design a house for them in Chicago, but after just seven years they sold the Mississippi property. The photograph here, one of few of the structure, was taken before 1910, and it is believed that the stables burned soon after. Subsequent owners have no recollection of the building, although the main bungalow and guesthouse have survived.

509 East Beach Road

Ocean Springs,

Mississippi

(top right)

Designed in 1890

Burned around 1911

SULLIVAN STABLES

In return for designing a vacation retreat for the Charnleys, Sullivan received five of their twenty-one acres in Ocean Springs and purchased six more. Here he built his own vacation home, servants quarters, and stables, which Wright claimed to have designed completely. The footprint of the stables was a miniature of the main cottage, a T shape with a polygonal bay on each end of the cross. Like the Charnley stables (see page 84), it was designed in the Shingle Style and was both austere and picturesque. The building had living quarters at one end and a front porch. In between this and the two-stall stables with a hayloft was a carriage house, entered through a large arch.

The long, narrow property ran from the Davis Bayou beachfront to a salt marsh in the rear. Sullivan created a landscape plan as curvilinear and free-flowing as his designs for architectural ornament. He loved the interaction with nature and benefited from the climate and the solitude he found among the azaleas and loblolly pine, gum, maple, hickory, dogwood, and plum trees. During the twenty years he owned the site, Sullivan spent as much time there as he could, continuously enhancing the gardens and cultivating one hundred rose species. An octagonal water tower on the back of the house, later converted into a wine cellar, predates Wright's octagonal library at his Oak Park studio (1898) and the one he designed for the Frederick Bagley house (1894) in Hinsdale, Illinois. His interest in semidetached octagonal forms may be rooted here.

The Sullivan cottage, thought to be less finely executed than the Charnley cottage, has been restored. The stables, however, outlived their usefulness, were left to deteriorate, and finally were demolished in 1942.

85

100 Holcomb Boulevard

Ocean Springs, Mississippi

(bottom left)

Designed in 1890

Demolished in 1942

WALLIS BOATHOUSE

That yearning of city dwellers to escape in the summer and head for the country became a reality for more and more wealthy families in the late 1890s as transportation options expanded. At the turn of the century Delavan Lake, not far from Milwaukee, was accessible from Chicago by four trains a day in the summer. Henry Wallis, an Oak Park real estate investor, purchased and subdivided a large tract of land on the lake, creating an impressive enclave that would eventually include many Wright-designed buildings.

Before he commissioned Wright to design his own vacation home in 1900, Wallis asked the architect to create a boathouse. The only known photograph of this structure is not available for publication, but the boathouse reportedly had a twenty-four-foot square base with boat storage below. Above was a central fifteen-foot square supported by L-shaped wing walls surrounded by a sheltered walkway. Beneath a hipped roof, an open railing encircled a viewing and picnic area on four sides. Covered in horizontal boards and battens like the later house, it rested naturally in the side of a hill at the water's edge.

Wright also designed a gatehouse, gates, and a sign for the entrance to the property, but it is unclear whether the gatehouse now standing is Wright's design. Many mysteries still remain about Wright's pre-1900 involvement with this project. The sign bracket with an iron circle of Isis is still there, but the gates are gone. The two fences, which extended forty-five degrees from the gatehouse, had wooden slats with balls and were marked by fieldstone piers with caps similar to those at Wright's home and studio (1889–98) in Oak Park. The gate was made of wooden slats with a rotated square cut in the panels.

On completion of his house, Wallis sold the property to the Goodsmith brothers, Heder M. and William P., two Chicago doctors whose wives were twins, and they altered it immediately. It has been changed many times since, and for a number of years the property was abandoned and suffered serious deterioration. The boathouse was demolished sometime before 1939. Although the house has since been restored and is in good condition, its early supporting structures have disappeared.

3409 South Shore Drive

Delavan, Wisconsin

Designed in 1897

Demolished before 1939

86

JONES BOATHOUSE

3335 South Shore Drive

Delavan, Wisconsin

(below)

Designed in 1900

Boathouse burned

in 1975; water tower

demolished in 1988

One investor who bought land from Henry Wallis around Delavan Lake was Fred Jones, an officer in a Chicago company that made brass fittings for Pullman rail cars. A bachelor who entertained frequently, he would have horse-drawn buses pick up his guests at the Delavan railroad station and deliver them to his country house for a weekend of recreation, which would undoubtedly center around activities on the water. The estate Wright designed for him in 1900, Penwern, was the most elaborate of the commissions on the lake.

The boathouse, like that for Wallis (see page 86), had boat storage below and a stairway to a partially covered pavilion above. Built into the side of the hill, it provided a great viewing area for activities on the lake. The clapboard-covered structure had fieldstone piers, a gabled roof, a low, flat-arch entry, and diamond-paned art glass like the main house. The roof's structural cross-beams were exposed, as they often were in recreation properties. The boathouse was an important component of the property, which included greenhouses, a water tower, a barn with stables, and a gatehouse, as well as the expansive residence with a billiard room, a card room in the tower, five bedrooms, and broad lawns.

The boathouse burned in 1975, and the water tower attached to the gatehouse was demolished in 1988. The latter had a tall fieldstone base with wood above and was topped by a gabled roof with an extended ridge like the main house. There is hope that the current owner will rebuild the boathouse using photographs and original plans.

WILDER STABLES

Before moving to Elmhurst in 1893, Thomas Edward Wilder had lived in Oak Park and was serving on the board of Unity Temple when the Wrights moved to town. A well-known promoter of public improvements, he was a successful tanner and wholesale leather merchant in Chicago.

Although the drawings for Wilder's stables came from Wright's studio, Walter Burley Griffin, who lived in Elmhurst, was responsible for the design. Griffin's independent projects outside Wright's office included the clubhouse for the Elmhurst Country Club (1901, demolished), which Wilder helped found, and the Emery house (1901) for Wilder's daughter, which had gabled roofs with flat extensions and wall surface divisions similar to the stables. Wright was yet to use these forms.

Like the Waller stables (see page 51), designed the same year, the Wilder stables were decidedly horizontal and had a two-story component housing an employee above the carriage room. Long stretches of plaster walls were cleanly delineated with extensive wood trim, particularly the second-story portion, which had an English half-timbered feeling. The built-in box gutters and divided-pane windows added substance to the structure.

The stables included a large poultry wing as well as stalls for horses and cows. Plaster-covered walls fenced in the barnyard, and tall triangular pylons served as vents for the manure shed. An early study shows a greenhouse extending in the other direction. Great care was given to the design, as evidenced by the several pages of drawings carefully addressing each detail.

In 1905 Wilder purchased a large 1860s house across from this site and lived there until his death in 1919. His house was later given to the City of Elmhurst and has served as its public library since 1922. Some of the estate grounds are a public park, but the site of the stables, demolished in 1941, is now part of Elmhurst College.

Prospect Avenue

at Elm Park

Elmhurst, Illinois

Designed in 1901

Demolished in 1941

88

FRICKE GARDEN PAVILION

The house designed for William G. Fricke was one of the few commissions that Wright completed while in partnership with Webster Tomlinson. It was sold five years later to Emma Martin, who had Wright design a garage in 1907 and who lived in the house until 1915. Sited on the far northern edge of the suburban lot, it opened generously to a garden to the south, a favored technique of Wright's that maximized the advantages of sunlight and avoided the limitations of a confined site.

The massive three-story stucco walls of the street side of the house communicated a sense of protection and privacy, while the multiple casement windows and detached garden pavilion opened the opposite side to the freedom of the natural world. Establishing these opposing forces was to become one of Wright's most distinctive tools, but here it was a technique he was just beginning to define effectively.

The garden pavilion was connected to the house by a covered passageway entered from the hall between the living and dining rooms. Open, with half walls of stucco like the house, it was sheltered by a low, hipped roof with broad overhangs. Corner piers were stepped back and flanked by columns similar to those dividing the windows of the house. A stairway led to the lawn below and the shade of a large oak tree. Another porch extended the three-story house to the east, providing access to the garden from another direction. If Wright provided an elaborate garden plan, it was not completely executed.

In 1928 the garden pavilion was demolished so that the side lot could be sold. The house built there closed the view to the south, completely changing the character of the Fricke house. While the interior spaces remain harmonious, the house lacks the dynamism that the openness of the pavilion and larger lot contributed.

540 Fair Oaks Avenue

Oak Park, Illinois

Designed in 1901

Demolished in 1928

DARWIN MARTIN GARAGE AND CoNSERVAToRY

The house that Wright designed for Darwin and Isabel Martin in 1904 was one of the architect's greatest achievements. Its significance derives from the close relationship between architect and client, the unity and poetry of the design, and the comprehensiveness of the site plan. The soul of the house was nature. Abstracted natural forms sparkled in the delicate art glass windows and the glass mosaic facing the fireplace. An important element in this masterful composition was a conservatory connected to the main house through a long pergola, which served as the intermediary between the natural and the built worlds.

The pergola, covered with a low, hipped roof, was entered near the dining room. The enclosed walkway of brick and art glass became a long, protected path through the gardens to the back of the property. Nature performed on all sides, pouring from planters, climbing garden walls, and blooming in the gardens beyond. At the end of the pergola was a cruciform-shaped conservatory designed as an indoor garden for the Martins to enjoy in addition to their greenhouse. It opened to the garden on one side and to the garage on the other. Not totally satisfied with its functionality, the Martins considered turning it into a tea room some years after they moved into the house.

Darwin D. and William E. Martin were entrepreneurs, partners in a shoe and stove polish company, among other ventures. William, who lived in Oak Park, introduced Wright to his brother, for whom the young architect would design an estate, a summer house, and the revolutionary administration building for the Larkin Company (see pages 132–37) in Buffalo, New York.

The Darwin Martin house began its decline in 1929, when Martin lost his fortune in the stock market crash. After his death in 1935 the building stood vacant for seventeen years. It was then purchased by a family who stabilized the house but decided to sell part of the property for redevelopment. The pergola and conservatory had been vandalized and were crumbling, and the garage was considered too far from the house. Some brick was salvaged to make repairs, and surviving art glass windows were given away before the structures were demolished in 1959. Multistory apartment buildings were built on the site, destroying the continuity and integrity of Wright's grand opus.

125 Jewett Parkway

Buffalo, New York

Designed in 1904

Demolished in 1959

WILLIAM MARTIN PERGoLA AND GARDEN

William E. Martin was a pivotal client who provided the link to at least two dozen Wright commissions, the first of which was his own Oak Park house, built in 1903. In 1908 he purchased the adjoining lot and in 1909 commissioned Wright to design an elaborate formal garden and pergola.

Supported by stucco-covered piers trimmed in wood, the pergola stretched from the east side of the porch to the driveway on the southern property line. Near the end a walkway led to a large circle-within-a-square fish pond. All around, a profusion of flowers tumbled from garden beds and raised urns. Lattice panels projected from the pergola columns and fenced a bridge crossing the pond. The geometric plan of the garden was punctuated by a Richard Bock sculpture. Pathways led to garden benches that served as places of reflection. Partially protected by a privacy wall extending from the front of the house, it was a family wonderland.

Martin's house was divided into apartments for relatives in the 1930s and remained in family hands until 1942. Garden walls, beds, urns on piers, the pond, and part of the pergola also remained but in a wild, dilapidated condition. The pool was partially filled in to make it safer.

When the lot was sold for redevelopment in 1951, a surprising amount of effort was required to remove the elaborate, ten-foot-deep concrete foundations of the walls and pool. On the remaining side lot new owners have recently created a garden that is a miniature of the original—teasing the imagination to remember what once was.

94

636 North East Avenue

Oak Park, Illinois

Designed in 1909

Demolished by 1951

BRIGHAM GARAGE

Wright's design here was for a Prairie Style carriage house, which undoubtedly was converted into a garage as times changed. Located in the far northwestern corner of the property, it had hipped roofs over a central core with two projecting wings like the main house. The servants quarters and horse stalls were in the center, with the carriage-automobile room on one side and a covered paddock on the other.

Many questions still remain about this elusive structure—its materials, form, and date. Wright's drawings for the Brigham house were done in his Oak Park studio, which dates the design 1908–9 even though it was not built until 1915. Although no photograph has been found to confirm that the garage built was Wright's design, there is some supporting evidence that it was constructed and connected to the city water system in 1908, seven years before the house was erected. The concrete foundation was discovered by the current owners, Howard and Susan Solway-Siegel, who have also seen a corner of the structure in a historic photo. A 1938 Sanborn fire map also shows the outline of a building that matches Wright's floor plan.

Edmund Brigham was a passenger agent and later an executive with the Chicago Northwestern Railroad, which connected the village of Glencoe with Chicago. His house, built near those of other family members in Glencoe, has the distinction of being the first of Wright's poured-concrete houses. Wright's concept for an all-concrete house was first published in a 1907 *Ladies' Home Journal* under the title "A Fireproof House for $5,000," but most of those built using this plan were actually stucco over a wood frame. It is believed that when the garage was demolished in 1968, it was replaced by the existing cinder-block structure that leads to the house via a covered passageway.

790 Sheridan Road

Glencoe, Illinois

(top right)

Designed in 1908

Demolished in 1968

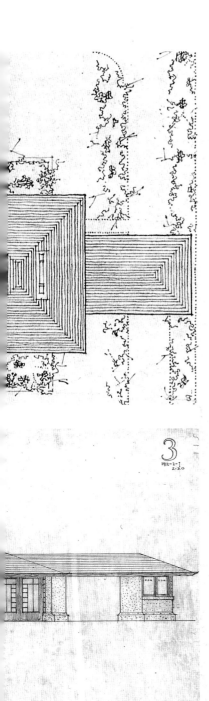

BooTH GARAGE AND STABLES

Sherman Booth was another of Wright's pivotal clients and for a while served as his attorney. He had purchased a farm in Glencoe and wanted to establish a subdivision there with houses of Wright's design. Many commissions would emanate from this relationship, which endured through Wright's greatest personal and professional turmoil, the period following the 1914 murders and fire at Taliesin.

The first buildings erected on the Booth property were a temporary cottage (1911, since moved) and a two-part garage and stables, designed in 1912. The garage sat at right angles to the stables and carriage wing and included a two-bedroom apartment for the resident caretaker and carpenter.

After designing the garage, Wright turned his attention to the main house, but the plans he submitted were too grandiose and beyond the Booths' budget. Work continued on the other houses in the development, as did plans for additional improvements. Eventually Wright created a revised, more realistic plan for the Booth house, which in 1916 obliterated the existing garage and stables by incorporating them into the residence.

In a 1979 letter Sherman Booth Jr. described these structures as single story and stucco with red tile roofs: "Wright's design incorporated the barn and gardeners cottage. The barn became the south kitchen/dining room wing, the cottage became the east study/bedroom wing. I remember the workmen knocking out the inside hollow tile partitions with sledge hammers in those two buildings for rearrangement of the rooms." The area between the two structures became the central core of the new house, containing the living room, the north porch, bedrooms, and a balcony on the second floor; a sleeping porch, lavatory, and roof garden on the third floor; and an open tower on the fourth floor over the southwest stairwell, a tall flagpole rising above it. The house survives in excellent condition.

Booth's daughter Betty indicates that her father loaned Wright money so that he could also invest in the Booth development. When he could not get Wright to repay the loan, Booth ended their relationship—an unpleasant conclusion to a mutually enriching friendship.

265 Sylvan Road

Glencoe, Illinois

(bottom left)

Designed in 1912

Incorporated into

the house in 1916

RECREATION AND TRAVEL

By the beginning of the twentieth century, travel was all the rage among Americans. The western expansion of passenger rail systems, the growth of a good road system, and the rapid acceptance of the automobile opened up new destination opportunities. Journeys could be farther and more frivolous, not limited to business or family visits as were those made by horse and buggy. Prosperity plus this increased mobility led to the development of countless vacation houses, resorts, hotels, railroad stations, restaurants, and sporting and social clubs—all new architectural opportunities.

Wright's sympathy with nature and his simple horizontal designs, use of natural materials, and open floor plans suited such informal activities. His demolished leisure-time buildings mirror the types of facilities being constructed and chronicle the range of his commissions. Large and small, city and country, single buildings and complex developments, they added a fascinating dimension to his creative output. Some of his most inventive and elaborate designs were never executed, however, most notably the Cheltenham Beach (1895) and Wolf Lake (ca. 1902) resort projects for the Chicago developer Edward C. Waller; the Nakoma Country Club (1923) in Madison, Wisconsin; and San Marcos-in-the-Desert (1929) in Chandler, Arizona, for Alexander Chandler.

Many of Wright's recreational designs were built outside large cities and with inexpensive materials, generally wood, such as Wisconsin's Delavan Lake Yacht Club (left), gone since 1916. Because most were seasonal structures, they were taken less seriously and thus were vulnerable to deterioration and changing fads. Some were created for new clubs that either failed or flourished, resulting in the original structure's obsolescence. Others, although large and solidly built, suffered from changing economic conditions and tastes. Consequently, a disproportionate number—two-thirds—of Wright-related recreation and travel buildings have been lost. The only survivors—none in its original form—are the River Forest Tennis Club (1906) in River Forest, Illinois; the lobby of the Imperial Hotel (1915) in Tokyo; the remaining structures of the Arizona Biltmore Hotel (1926) in Phoenix and of Como Orchards (1909) in Darby, Montana; and the Riverview Restaurant (1953) in Spring Green, Wisconsin, now the Taliesin Visitors Center.

VICToRIA HoTEL

While Wright was employed by Adler and Sullivan, the office was given the commission for the Victoria Hotel in Chicago Heights. George Grant Elmslie, an associate at the time, reported that Wright was responsible for much of the design. Commissioned by Victor Faulkenau, the hotel was completed in anticipation of the throngs of people expected to descend on Chicago for the World's Columbian Exposition in 1893. Located near the Indiana border, Chicago Heights was a convenient resting place for those traveling into the city.

Unfortunately, only one visitor to the fair registered at the hotel. Nonetheless the architectural landmark became the hub of social and cultural activities in the industrial town for many years. Distinguished out-of-town guests were often entertained at the Victoria, and most of the prominent bachelors in Chicago Heights resided here.

Modeled after Adler and Sullivan's Opera House (1889) in Pueblo, Colorado, the lower two floors were of red brick veneer over a wood frame and were marked by a massive, richly ornamented entrance arch. The third floor and the distinctive clock tower were covered with yellow staff, an ornamental plaster precast in geometric patterns and strengthened with fiber. The 105 guest rooms were augmented with shops, a bank, a billiards room, a bar, and a large rotunda. With its steam heat, hot and cold water, electric lights, exceptional service, and fine cuisine, the Victoria was considered a first-class hotel. The interiors were conventionally Victorian, showing no evidence of Wright's involvement.

The surface ornament, hipped roofs, and broad overhangs predate Wright's carefully composed design for the Winslow house in River Forest the following year but share the Sullivanesque massing, clear geometry, and stylized integral ornament seen in the collaborations for the Charnley house (1891) and Sullivan house (1891) (see pages 42–43), both in Chicago.

The building was not solidly built and suffered deterioration. A 1934 remodeling eliminated most of the distinctive arches on the hotel's main floor and significantly altered the dining room and lobby. Various businesses continued to occupy the main floor after the hotel was closed to guests in 1958. Awaiting demolition to make way for a shopping center, it was gutted by a fire three years later. The site is now a parking lot.

West End Avenue

at Vincennes Avenue

(formerly 69

Illinois Street)

Chicago Heights,

Illinois

Designed in 1892

Burned in 1961

ROCKY ROOST

Wright's childhood friend Robert Lamp (known as Robie) was linked in some way to nearly all the architect's early Madison projects. Politically active, he was in the insurance, real estate, and travel businesses and had many connections. Lamp and Melville Clarke discovered that a small island in Madison's Lake Mendota had not been identified and was therefore not known to be public property. In 1892 they arranged to buy it cheaply, build three small cabins on it, and use it as a recreation destination. Close-to-home country retreats were popular at the time, and the location appealed to the owners' mutual love of boating.

In 1902 the owners decided to improve the property. Wright helped them coordinate a new design for the existing buildings, which were simple frame structures that some believe Wright may even have designed. The three were drawn together and reworked into a single unit, and a second story with a wraparound porch was added. The porch projected beyond the lower floor and was supported by wooden posts and brackets. A three-part, low-pitched terra-cotta–colored roof covered all, creating a unified structure for entertaining and sleeping that became known as Rocky Roost. The clapboards and Stick Style trim were painted in shades of grays and greens to blend with the surrounding flora. A yellow brick chimney rose above. A windmill, added the following year to bring well water to the site, contributed both a viewing tower and a greater sense of substance.

Among the many visitors to the site were Mamah and Edwin Cheney, Wright clients from Oak Park whose marriage Wright helped break up when he ran off with Mamah in 1909. Lamp died in 1916, and the fragile assemblage burned down eighteen years later. The tiny spit of land on which it stood is now often under water.

Northwest of

Governors Island

Lake Mendota

Madison, Wisconsin

Designed in 1892;

redesigned in 1902

Burned in 1934

103

LAKE MENDoTA BoATHOUSE

To clean up the shorelines and improve the appearance of Madison's many lakes, the Madison Improvement Association was formed in 1893. It announced a competition for designs for community boathouses to replace the ramshackle structures scattered along the beach. Wright probably heard about the contest from his friend Robie Lamp. A pair of his designs won and became two of his earliest independent commissions. The Lake Monona Boathouse was never built because of the 1893 depression, but the Lake Mendota Boathouse was completed by the end of that year at a cost of $3,100.

With its dual pavilions in reddish brown wood and cream-colored plaster, the graceful, thirty-two-foot-high building was a noble addition to the shoreline. Built into a steep slope, the boathouse provided a large curved viewing platform above a boat storage and launching area. The sweep of its wooden shingle forms fit neatly into the residential neighborhood, repeating the Shingle Style characteristics of the house next door. The arcade, the large arched boat entry, the battered walls, and the broad eaves reflected Wright's recently completed apprenticeship with Louis Sullivan, but the carefully balanced, geometric composition, with its low, hipped roofs, was uniquely Wright's.

The boat bay and storage area provided berths in two semicircular tiers, each of which held fourteen boats and could be reached by a unique pivoting crane from an overhead track. A sheltered area at the boat bay entrance provided protection for those getting on and off their boats.

By the mid-1920s neighbors were complaining about the building's poor condition. They were granted permission to dismantle the boathouse in 1926, and the owners of the adjoining properties gained control of the valuable lakefront when the building was gone. No mention was made that it was a Wright design; the only publicly stated regret was the loss of boat storage space and bait sales.

Carroll Street

near Langdon Avenue

Madison, Wisconsin

Designed in 1893

Demolished in 1926

104

RIVER FOREST GoLF CLUB

In 1898 Wright designed a clubhouse for a nine-hole private golf course built less than a mile from his Oak Park home and studio. Land for this community enhancement was made available by the realtor Edmund A. Cummings. Despite its brief life of seven years, the clubhouse provided a pivotal preview of Wright's later Prairie Style dwellings and country retreats. In the words of the architectural historian Henry-Russell Hitchcock, the River Forest Golf Club was "not a mere Opus I, but a First Symphony. If the essential character of its construction and design, so closely integrated as to be inseparable, can be understood, almost all the work of the first decade of Wright's maturity will fall into place."

The original board-and-batten front wing had many features identified with Wright's later designs. With its low, hipped roofs and continuous bands of windows with wooden mullions, the emphasis was clearly horizontal. Large urns marked the front entrance, and a massive masonry chimney anchored the composition, whose spaciousness extended to the outside terraces.

The early plan was simple: an assembly room, changing rooms, and a large porch. Three years later the clubhouse was greatly expanded by Wright, who added an octagonal lounge with two fireplaces. The compatible addition had a symmetrical plan with a large dining room on one side of the foyer and locker rooms on the other.

In 1905 the club moved farther west to a larger site. Attempts to sell Wright's building failed, so it was demolished that year. A portion of the land was donated to the River Forest Tennis Club, which in 1906 commissioned Wright (with Charles White and Vernon Watson) to design its building. This clubhouse was moved in 1920. A third Wright-designed building stood briefly on the land when Cummings built his real estate office here in 1905 (see page 138), but it was demolished in 1925 after the property was sold to the Cook County Forest Preserve.

Bonnie Brae Avenue

near Quick Street

River Forest, Illinois

Designed in 1898;

remodeled in 1901

Demolished in 1905

DELAVAN LAKE YACHT CLUB

By 1890 the Oak Park real estate developer Henry Wallis acquired property on the south end of Delavan Lake, built his own house there, and offered other lots for sale to wealthy Chicagoans for their summer homes. Just seventy miles from the city and served by several trains, it quickly became a popular resort community. Five elaborate Wright-designed houses with multiple outbuildings were eventually built at the lake.

Wallis commissioned Wright to design a yacht club nearby, which would become the center of sporting and social activities. The T-shaped building with shallow, hipped roofs and diamond-paned leaded glass had a horizontal presentation with distinctive flagpoles that rose like spires and added a vertical counterpoint. A small, casual, dark-stained, board-and-batten structure built next to the water's edge, its architectural form was similar to one used by Wright on many rustic commissions following the River Forest Golf Club (1898, 1901) (see pages 106–7).

The clubhouse had a central space for dancing, a dining area on one side, and a ladies' parlor on the opposite side. Fires built in the massive fireplace with a distinctive flat-arch opening warmed the space on cool evenings. A terrace, as large as the dance floor and partially covered, extended across the front of the building, offering good views of activities on the lake. Stairways led from both sides to the dock below, and a long pier served as the docking area for the frequent sailboat races.

In 1915 a larger clubhouse, not designed by Wright, was built directly south of the yacht club, and Wright's smaller one was demolished the following year. The larger building is now a private home, and both sites are part of the Delmar subdivision. A park providing the residents access to the lake is located at the old yacht club site.

Approximately 2805

South Shore Drive

Delavan, Wisconsin

(top right)

Designed in 1902

Demolished in 1916

FOX RIVER CoUNTRY CLUB

Clients drawn to the revolutionary architect were often revolutionary in their own right, but for eccentricity none could surpass Col. George Fabyan. A wealthy textile manufacturer and scientist, he commissioned Wright in 1907 to remodel an existing Italianate house into a private country club.

Fabyan preferred entertaining famous international dignitaries on his exotic estate rather than traveling himself. The club was also intended to be a popular motoring destination, offering croquet, golf, swimming, canoeing, tennis, and theater in the summer and dancing, bowling, billiards, and card parties in the winter. It had fourteen overnight rooms and was served by an interurban trolley. "Nowadays," stated the club brochure, "a community is not modern unless it has a country club."

As an addition on the house's north side, Wright designed a long, low, gabled structure with wood siding and a broad chimney. It housed a thirty-by-seventy-five-foot dance hall with large exposed trusses and Prairie Style divided plaster walls. A bowling alley and billiards tables were a level below. Running the length of the addition was a veranda with many windows and doors opening onto it; an overhanging roof protected all. Gravel walks wound through the grounds of the rambling wooded site.

Fabyan had sixty to seventy employees who worked on the estate and studied subjects as diverse as Japanese gardens, cryptology, Shakespeare, levitation, acoustics, tuning forks, medical instruments, and philosophy. He also had bears, alligators, exotic birds, a fake mummy, Roman pools, a dairy, chickens, grain, greenhouses, and an amphitheater that seated 1,200.

The clubhouse burned to the ground in an early morning fire in 1910. It is believed that housing for workers on the estate and a dining hall called the Grille were built on the old foundations.

Route 31

south of Forest Avenue

Geneva, Illinois

(bottom left)

Designed in 1907

Burned in 1910

CoMo ORCHARDS CLUB-HOUSE AND CoTTAGES

Como Orchards was a land development scheme inspired by the western rail-road expansion. By 1909 three rail lines ran to Missoula, Montana, and when the Northern Pacific connected a spur south to the Bitter Root Valley, transportation of people and products became increasingly easy. The establishment of the Bitter Root irrigation district and construction of the Lake Como Dam and the Big Ditch Canal, both financed by the Chicago investor W. I. Moody and supervised by F. D. Nichols, enabled promoters to attract new investors with hopes of establishing a huge apple-growing industry in the valley.

The first development of their Bitter Root Valley Irrigation Company was the 1,600-acre University Heights, created by the subsidiary Como Orchards Land Company. The plan was to sell ten-acre orchard plots plus a building site for $4,000. The company would care for the trees and in five years, when they would start bearing fruit, it would market the produce for ten percent of the profit. The promoters targeted college professors, particularly those from the University of Chicago, who might wish to spend summers in the "most unusual combination of civilization and rugged mountain wilderness—where orchard and forest reserve meet." This appeal to an intellectual, urban elite was a unique marketing strategy at the time.

Wright was asked to design the master plan, clubhouse, land office building, and cottages. He visited the site in 1909, but it is believed that Marion Mahony and William Drummond in his office supervised the project. All the buildings were board and batten. The clubhouse had a two-story lounge and a large dining room with vast, open porches and three large stone fireplaces. The bedroom wing was on the opposite side of the long, narrow plan.

At least fifty-three cottages were originally planned around the clubhouse, but only twelve were constructed. The small frame structures had stone fireplaces but were built cheaply as seasonal, camplike housing, with no central heat and pine blocks instead of foundations. The two-bedroom cottages had no kitchen space, while the three-bedroom versions had a kitchen and porch.

The unpredictable weather and enormous shipping problems caused the project to fail. The bank foreclosed in 1916, and even Wright lost money. Several cottages stood until the late 1930s; others were gradually torn down. The clubhouse was altered, whitewashed, and used to house workers and store hog feed. In 1945 the boards were taken to build a barn. Now only the abandoned land office building and one three-bedroom cottage remain.

469 Bunkhouse Road

Darby, Montana

Designed in 1909

Demolished 1930–45

BITTER ROOT INN

In addition to the Como Orchards project, Wright designed a second development for the Bitter Root Valley Irrigation Company—a town plan and an inn for Bitter Root, which was located at the northern end of the hundred-mile-long irrigation district. Wright's first grand scheme, drafted in early 1909, was based on a grid with buildings in each square surrounding an inner court. A central green space adjoined all the community service buildings, with the inn at the head of the park. The plan included a depressed rail line that was covered where roads and walkways crossed it. Wright was also asked later that year to design a smaller village plan and a few buildings for the village center. Neither plan was implemented.

The only structure actually built was the Bitter Root Inn. Potential investors from the East were brought by the trainload and lavishly entertained at the inn. Similar to the clubhouse at Como Orchards (see pages 110–11), it was a horizontal board-and-batten building, 126 feet long, with a full-length veranda. It was sited to take advantage of the good view toward Harriet Park on the west and the orchards to the south. The T-shaped structure had a

Porter Hill

at Eastside Highway

Stevensville, Montana

Designed in 1909

Burned in 1924

low-pitched, shingled roof and eighteen camplike rooms with a shared bathroom and a central dining room. A ribbon of divided-glass windows ran beneath the roof.

Bitter Root was intended to be an attractive, rural mountain community surrounded by acres of orchards, boasting "a pine-covered ridge, wooded ravines, good drainage, good elevation, and picturesque views." Compatible house plans were available at the company offices. Those illustrated on Wright's master plan look like square designs with boards and battens, similar to those he created for a Chicago subdivision proposed by Edward C. Waller that year. The company hoped that the appearance of all the buildings would be harmonious, in keeping with Wright's compelling desire to create a unified whole.

Water and power plants were installed to serve a town of one thousand, but the community never found its footing. The company's bankruptcy in 1916 halted all development. The inn was used for classrooms and then as a dance hall until it burned in 1924. A road now passes through the site.

WALLER BATHING PAVILION

In 1880 the real estate developer Edward C. Waller, Wright's old friend, bought two thousand acres of land between Lake Michigan and Lake Charlevoix. A well-known advocate of reforestation, he replanted the property with thousands of pine trees to replace what had been clear-cut during the lumbering boom of the preceding years. Waller was one of the earliest members of the Chicago Club, formed in 1880, to which he donated part of his land for a golf course. Although he envisioned building a large Wright-designed summer home there for himself, only a large swimming pavilion for changing and socializing was constructed, built on sixty-four feet of Lake Michigan shoreline three miles from the club.

Wright's design was similar to the Delavan Lake Yacht Club of 1902 in Wisconsin (see page 108). The board-and-batten structure had a large front terrace with a central common room. The ladies' and gentlemen's parlors were on either side, and a service area was in the rear.

The horizontal building sat above the rocky shore on a sand dune. Beneath the hipped roof were exposed rafters, which continued beneath the eaves. The simple structural elements were not concealed with plaster or paneling as they would have been in a residence. The bow-tie pattern in the windows, similar to that in the Ingalls house (1909) in River Forest, Illinois, and the Bradley house (1901), in Kankakee, Illinois, repeated the angle of the roofline and its structural members.

Charlevoix had been connected to Chicago by a passenger rail line since 1892. The Chicago Resort Special and a steamer line made commuting to the lake convenient, so it became a popular retreat. But Waller's bathing pavilion was located in a remote area and vacant most of the time. It was converted into a residence before being destroyed by a fire. According to local lore, the house became a popular trysting spot, which may have helped bring Wright's work here to a passionate end. A new house stands in its place.

114

12615 Pa Ba Shan Lane

Charlevoix, Michigan

(top right)

Designed in 1909

Burned in 1922 or 1923

CHICAGo NORTH SHORE— MILWAUKEE STATION

The attorney Sherman Booth's vision for a residential development in the Chicago suburb of Glencoe was a comprehensive one that included many public structures, not just houses. From 1911 to 1915 Wright worked with Booth to create a community unified in design. A bridge, planters, sculptures, seven houses, and a train station were built, contributing to the integrated plan that Booth sought. A founder of the Glencoe Park District, Booth was hopeful that Wright could also provide other improvements for the growing eight-acre community, such as a town hall, an art gallery, and other train stations. It was a turbulent, transitional time in Wright's life, and Booth's friendship, legal services, and patronage were of great value to him.

Long thought never built, the Chicago North Shore—Milwaukee railway waiting station was actually one of two ideas that Wright provided and shares stylistic features with his proposed Yahara Boathouse (1905) for Madison, Wisconsin. Each had a flat, cantilevered roof over solid plaster or cement walls and sat on an extended platform. The simple, small shelter in Glencoe included a covered outside portion and an enclosed heated room. Horizontal planes sandwiched the core of the building, unifying the voids and the solids. Its abstract simplicity was compatible with the other buildings in the Booth development and was more unusual than Wright's alternative hipped-roof design. In contrast, the wooden train station he proposed for Banff Park (1911) in Alberta, Canada, was rustic, in keeping with the character of that site.

The new electric railway system that served the station connected downtown Chicago with the northern suburbs and eventually Milwaukee, certainly an asset to Booth's development plans. The Booth property ran to the electric railway tracks, which paralleled the Chicago Northwestern tracks. The station sat on a small triangle of land next to a park that extended to Meadow Road. A path led the way from the Booth enclave, making the commute a simple one.

The electric train service was discontinued in the mid-1950s, and all the stations were demolished. A bike trail that follows the old rail bed passes the now-empty site of the station.

Greenbay Road crossing

at Franklin Road

Glencoe, Illinois

(bottom left)

Designed in 1911

Demolished in

the mid-1950s

BANFF PAVILION

One-fourth mile west

of the south end

of Banff Avenue Bridge

Banff, Alberta, Canada

Designed in 1911

Demolished in 1938

Francis C. Sullivan, an eccentric, temperamental architect from Ottawa, joined the Chicago studio of Wright, his hero, for a few months in 1911. Armed with political connections in the Department of Public Works, he enticed Wright into collaborating on several Canadian projects as "F. L. Wright and F. C. Sullivan, Associated Architects." Their lives continued to intertwine until Sullivan's death in 1929.

The Banff Pavilion is the only collaborative structure that was built. Wright prepared the design, and Sullivan did the working drawings and supervised the project, maintaining contact with Wright's office in Chicago. Built near the Bow River in 1914 for $20,000, the building was surrounded by athletic grounds and was intended as a motoring destination, a recreation center, and a dance hall for the residents of Banff.

Similar in appearance to the Como Orchards and Bitter Root projects (see pages 110–13), it was a long, narrow (200 by 50 feet), dark-stained, one-story building of rough-sawn wood on a stone foundation. Wright referred to the pavilion as a more substantial version of the River Forest Tennis Club (1906). It had a central lounge with three distinctive cobblestone fireplaces, a ladies' lounge on one end, and a men's on the other. The plan terminated with rotated squares on each end. The supporting trusses were exposed, and the light fixtures attached to the beams were custom designed. A continuous ribbon of floor-to-ceiling art glass windows with a chevron pattern opened the building to one side, while on the other an inglenook enclosed the cozy fireplace.

Problems arose with this project from the beginning, when the Canadian government's engineers challenged the sturdiness of the building, particularly the long spans, and demanded structural tests. Some citizens who wanted a hockey and curling rink considered the pavilion useless. For a while it was used as a quartermaster's store and then as an inconvenient place to wait for trains (the station was a mile away). The biggest problem was the site's swampiness; the floods of 1920 and 1933 caused serious damage. Although some groups in Calgary and Banff protested, the building was demolished in 1938, and the marshy Bow River has obliterated all traces of it.

RECREATION GROUNDS. BANFF.

RECREATION GROUNDS BANFF

LAKE GENEVA HoTEL

Lake Geneva's close proximity to both Chicago and Milwaukee made it a popular early-twentieth-century motoring destination for city dwellers. This ready clientele motivated the businessman John Williams and the Milwaukee developer Arthur L. Richards to join forces and form the Lake Geneva Hotel Company. In announcing plans for this new hotel, the local newspaper reported that "the advent of the automobile has revolutionized travel and made hotels of this character a practical necessity in any town which pretends to cater to the traveling public."

Commissioned in 1911, soon after Wright returned from his year in Europe, the design was a transitional one—crisply geometric with dominant, Prairie Style features. Wright's horizontal plan called for a 360-foot-long main building with ninety rooms, generous terraces, and a three-story wing of suites at one end. The suites were omitted, however—one of many changes made to the original plans as the building was being constructed.

Light-colored stucco walls beneath a stretched hipped roof were broken by bands of windows, and wood banding defined the openings. A large fireplace in the lobby had a semicircular arch created by long, tapered bricks and a flat metal sculpture. Dominant earth tones of green and brown were accented by touches of red in the art glass windows. The dining room light fixtures were simple clusters of offset, rectangular, art glass boxes around a coffered art glass skylight ceiling. Square glass wall sconces separated banks of windows. The upper-window glass pattern used an angular tulip motif, while the lower fixed panels repeated the rectangular forms. Primarily clear, they had touches of opalescent and iridescent glass.

Within two years of its opening in late 1912, the hotel had developed financial troubles. As its ownership changed frequently, the building continued to deteriorate and was altered several times. Finally, after a fire in one wing, it was demolished in 1970. A high-rise condominium development stands in its place.

Near the Lake Geneva

outlet and lagoon

between Broad and

Center Streets

Lake Geneva, Wisconsin

Designed in 1911

Demolished in 1970

PARK RIDGE CoUNTRY CLUB ADDITION

In 1906 a group of citizens founded the Park Ridge Country Club for "good fellowship, the promotion of golf, lawn tennis, field games, athletic sports—social features." They already had tennis courts, so for $500 a year they leased a nearby farm, where they coaxed a nine-hole golf course out of the corn fields. In 1911 they purchased this land for $300 an acre, expanded the course to a cramped eighteen holes, and soon commissioned Wright to remodel the farmhouse into an attractive clubhouse.

The design emanated from Wright's Chicago office and was signed off on by Wright's son John Lloyd Wright, who was working with him at the time. According to the plan, two existing farm buildings were connected by glazed and screened porches with trees growing through the roofs. The board-and-batten structure had an open dancing area with a terrace embellished with trellises and continuous flower boxes. A curved cement pool extended into the courtyard. According to club history, the buildings' "countrified atmosphere and unique beauty . . . became known far and wide." Members could take the train from Chicago to the Park Ridge station and be shuttled to the club by a special horse-drawn wagon.

The grounds continued to be improved and expanded. Trees and shrubs were planted at each hole on the golf course, and three hundred birdhouses were scattered around the site. The farm buildings had been converted into the men's and women's locker rooms, but the club lacked modern conveniences such as showers and heat. The amenities were actually so inadequate that the board meetings were usually held elsewhere. In 1922 members decided that they must have a new clubhouse. Designed by Schmidt, Garden and Martin, it opened three years later.

The old clubhouse with the Wright-designed addition remained on the east side of the parking lot and was used as a caddy shack. Sometime before 1930 it was torn down to make way for a new caddy shack and dormitory.

120

North Prospect Avenue

near Sibley Street

Park Ridge, Illinois

Designed in 1912

Demolished by 1930

MIDWAY GARDENS

Cottage Grove Avenue

at 60th Street

Chicago

Designed in 1913

Demolished in 1929

122

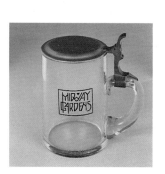

In the heart of industrial Chicago, Wright designed an exotic fantasy. Midway Gardens, a world-class, European-style entertainment center, was a magical complex that integrated the visual and performing arts with distinctive architecture. Tragically, like a dream, it was destined for a short life.

The client, Edward C. Waller Jr., son of Wright's friend and patron Edward C. Waller, was impressed by the popularity of outdoor concert gardens in Europe. Wright, also aware of this phenomenon, agreed to design this ambitious complex. The creative team included the sculptors Alfonso Ianelli and Richard Bock, three painters, the engineer Paul Mueller, and the site superintendent John Lloyd Wright, the architect's son. Years later John described how in just one hour the entire project was transferred from his father's mind to paper.

The outdoor Summer Garden on the west end of the complex had a large orchestra shell and seven hundred seats. Tables and chairs filled the surrounding court and balconies. At the east end the three-story Winter Garden provided space for indoor concerts, dining, and dancing during colder weather. The Tavern, on the north side, and Midway Garden Club, on the south side, allowed for more intimate gatherings and offered special services to members.

A plethora of two- and three-dimensional geometric designs interplayed exuberantly throughout the composition, creating a visual symphony. Against a linear backdrop of yellow brick and cast-concrete walls, Ianelli's sprites marched around the sunken garden, winged figures trumpeted the entrance to the Winter Garden and band shell, and spires of cubes rose like notes of a melody. Abstract murals on the Tavern walls developed the circle as a minor theme, while triangles in the art glass tapped a response. Wright-designed lamps and tableware enhanced the gourmet dining, while renowned performers entertained. It was a grand opus—a feast for the senses.

To open in June 1914 the National Symphony Orchestra played three concerts each evening, and famous dancers such as Anna Pavlova performed. The entrance fee was twenty-five cents, season tickets $10. Despite its instant popularity, Midway Gardens closed within two years. Waller's investment of $65,000 fell far short of the $350,000 needed to pay the bills, and he filed for bankruptcy in 1916. The property was sold to a brewery, which greatly modified the structure and used it as a beer garden and dance hall until 1928. After a difficult demolition in 1929, a gas station and a car wash were built on the site. Today only a small brick and concrete fragment of Midway Gardens remains in the alley behind the public housing that now occupies the site.

IMPERIAL HoTEL

Wright's most extraordinary commission, the Imperial Hotel occupied the bulk of his energy for eight years, from 1915 to 1923. This unique project provided him an opportunity to intimately experience the country he had so long admired and translate his understanding of its culture into form.

When the hotel opened in 1923, *Shufuntomo* magazine boasted, "The new Imperial Hotel ... makes an unhesitating use of modern science and civilization.... In fact this grand hotel is attested to be without peer in Japan and the world." Louis Sullivan, Wright's mentor, declared in *Architectural Record* that the Imperial Hotel stood "unique as the high water mark thus far attained by any modern architect. Superbly beautiful as it stands—a noble prophecy."

The three-story masterpiece had two 500-foot-long wings with 285 guest rooms. The central core included a theater seating one thousand people, a cabaret, a banquet hall, and a formal dining room. Promenades 300 feet long connected the guest wings with the public spaces. The modern mechanical and electrical systems were hidden in the building's columns. A reflecting pool greeted entering guests, while inner garden courts provided a quiet refuge.

Art was integrated into the fabric of the building. The sculptural forms Wright had carved from volcanic oya stone were as much Mayan as Japanese. Murals, urns, carpets, furniture, and tableware were all designed as elements of the unified composition of textures, colors, and forms.

On September 1, 1923, just as the opening ceremony for the hotel began, the great Kanto earthquake struck, destroying three-quarters of Tokyo, setting 134 fires, and displacing 1.5 million residents. Because of the unique floating, reinforced-concrete foundation, which Wright and the engineer Paul Mueller had designed, the hotel remained standing, but it was damaged and its decline had begun.

The fire bombing of Tokyo in 1945 during World War II destroyed the banquet halls and south wing and exacerbated a sag in the central core. Repairs were not taken seriously, and the oya stone was whitewashed during the American occupation of Japan. By the 1960s only the lobby and a promenade remained in original condition. Rationalizations for demolition—the concealed mechanical systems were difficult to update for air conditioning and television, the wooden roofs did not meet new building codes—grew, along with the management's fears that the hotel was not the most economically productive use of the valuable center-city land. Finally the hotel was razed. The lobby was saved and rebuilt as part of the Meiji Mura outdoor museum near Nagoya. A new Imperial Hotel has risen in its place.

1-1-1 Uchisaiwai-cho

Chiyoda-ku

Tokyo

Designed in 1915

Demolished in 1968

127

ARIZONA BILTMORE CoTTAGES

The design for a luxury hotel in Phoenix was a collaboration between Wright and Albert McArthur, son of a former client and an apprentice in Wright's Oak Park studio twenty years earlier. Wright credited the Biltmore Hotel design to McArthur, whose brothers were active in promoting the Phoenix area as a tourist destination, explaining that he had served only in a consulting role and shared his textile-block technology for a fee. McArthur, however, never designed anything else of substance—leaving all who experience the resort to conclude that Wright's contribution was significant indeed.

Wright's unique textile blocks, a precast concrete-block system integrating decorative patterns into the material, was developed for his California houses of the 1920s. When published in 1927, the system captured the McArthurs' attention. Wright designed the hollow blocks to be used structurally, interwoven with steel bars and trapping air for insulation. With blocks cast on the site, the standardized system was meant to cut costs while enlivening a lowly material. For the hotel, however, the blocks were not used structurally as intended but as an ornamental covering over a wood structure. Wright lamented the changes made to his innovative building technique, "which soon robbed the system of all economic value and left it standing as a novel and beautiful outside for an unintelligent engineer inside." Twenty-nine types of block, eighteen by thirteen inches, were eventually cast in aluminum forms. The sculptor Emry Kopta assisted with the designs, which are believed to be based on musical instruments or an abstracted palm leaf.

Fifteen cottages were scattered around the landscaped site behind the main hotel. Simple structures with flat roofs, they were constructed primarily of plain blocks used structurally as intended. In his 1932 autobiography Wright observed that in the cottages "the details of the system itself were better followed with better results." Of the eleven one-story cottages, six had three bedrooms and five had five bedrooms. The four two-story versions had six bedrooms.

In 1983 the hotel management renovated and expanded the resort by adding Terrace Court, a 120-room building. Three one-story cottages on the north end, one small and two larger, were demolished to make room for the new structure. Other cottages were updated; old bathrooms were converted into bedrooms, and modern bathrooms were added. The main hotel building still welcomes visitors to the desert that became Wright's second home.

130

24th Street

at East Missouri Street

Phoenix

(top right)

Designed in 1927

Demolished in 1983

CHANDLER CAMP CABINS

Alexander Chandler's grand vision in 1929 for San Marcos-in-the-Desert, a luxury resort in Arizona, became the focus of Wright's studio at a time when he had few other commissions. Wright moved his office from Wisconsin to Chandler, Arizona, and worked with the developer on a variety of projects, the smallest of which was a farm camp, the only design that was built.

Chandler Heights was created nearby on part of the thirty square miles of land owned by the Chandler Improvement Company. Stretching seven miles along the Hunt Highway, it offered perfect citrus soil, climate, irrigation, and beautiful views. Tracts of land were sold to absentee investors who could participate in the growth of the orchard industry that still thrives in the area.

The citrus tract camp that Wright designed in 1929 for Chandler Heights Citrus, Inc., consisted of a dozen distinctive wooden buildings with canvas roofs. Basic but electrified, the camp was used by the manager as a residence and an office and had six sleeping boxes for visitors and workers, a recreation hall, a dining hall, and a kitchen building. First available in April 1929, they were constructed on wooden platforms built of two-by-fours, with board-and-batten walls and canvas roofs, similar to the cabins Wright had just built for his own entourage at Ocatilla (see pages 28–31). Two layers of canvas provided insulation. The unique roof design of the sleeping boxes used a triangular module to create a partial geodesic canopy at the entrance, with flaps that could open or close to allow air movement.

Chandler's fortunes changed drastically when the stock market crashed in 1929, and no other buildings were constructed. Much of the Chandler land was sold as he consolidated his resources. No one kept track of the simple cabins, and they were dismantled and gone by 1934.

Santan Mountains

Chandler Heights, Arizona

(bottom left)

Designed in 1929

Demolished by 1934

Although Wright spent his formative professional years from 1888 to 1893 in the Chicago offices of Adler and Sullivan, a firm known for its large commercial commissions, he became a residential specialist. Only five percent of his work—twenty-six projects—was business related. His hotels and apartments could be considered business ventures, but they were primarily living spaces, not working spaces.

In his commercial designs Wright revealed a special ability to apply spatial and decorative skills to problems posed by the workplace. His daring clients were willing to integrate Wright's experimental ideas into their public images, not just their private homes. Wright's stylistic grammar, straightforward use of materials, and uncanny sense of human space in commercial buildings paralleled features of his residential designs. But his desire to transfer his unconventional, humanistic principles to the business environment may have frightened away clients who wanted familiar, traditional forms. Those who took the risk and shared Wright's vision for an architecture that suited America were generally rewarded with favorable publicity.

One-third of Wright's commercial projects have been demolished by human acts, including his first, the revolutionary Larkin Administration Building (1903) in Buffalo, New York (right). That innovative structure became the prototype for other commercial designs, such as the Johnson Wax Administration Building (1936) in Racine, Wisconsin, built three decades later. His six commercial remodelings have subsequently been remodeled themselves, subject to ever-changing fashion. Of these, only the Rookery lobby (1905) in Chicago has been returned to Wright's design.

Two particularly unusual lost properties have gone unheralded: the Island Woolen Company Dam Observation Deck (1913) in Baraboo, Wisconsin, and the Blue Parrot Patio Tea Room (1934) in Oak Park, Illinois. Yet because they occurred at transitional—indeed, critical—periods of Wright's life, they reveal the workings of his office during those times. Others are less obscure but have not been studied as much as his residential work. With the exception of the Larkin Building, now an icon of unnecessary loss, Wright's destroyed commercial buildings have been relegated to footnotes and lists.

BUSINESSES

LARKIN ADMINISTRATION BUILDING

Darwin D. Martin, the secretary of the Larkin Company, saw Wright's work while visiting his brother William in Oak Park in 1902. Martin subsequently invited the architect to Buffalo, the home of the company's successful mail-order and direct-sales soap business. Wright was ultimately commissioned to design several houses in Buffalo as well as the offices for the Larkin Company.

The office building site—dirty, noisy, unattractive—was in Buffalo's industrial zone. Wright's design turned the building inward, creating a refuge for the workers, with spaces and furnishings suited to their tasks. The company's progressive managers, believing that a humane working environment would enhance workers' morale, offered their employees concerts, lectures, picnics, and low-interest loans.

The five-story, red brick building and its three-story annex were a monumental exercise in solid geometry, with spheres atop towering piers and blocklike corner stair towers. Relief panels and sculptures of geometric figures and forms were designed by Wright and the sculptor Richard Bock as integral elements of the structure. Fountains marked the entrance, and geometric patterns on oversized pier capitals drew the eye upward seventy-six feet to the top of the glass-roofed central court. Motivational quotations proclaiming the virtues of hard work were gilded onto balcony walls.

Within the interior of cream-colored brick, magnesite (a durable poured concrete and wood product) was used to cover desktops, countertops, and floors. Sphere-within-a-square light fixtures, used individually and clustered, were mounted on walls and posts or suspended from the ceiling. Metal furniture was custom designed for the record-keeping card system that Martin had devised; many desks had swing-away chairs. Wooden and upholstered furniture was designed for the lounge, library, and dining areas. Windows were hermetically sealed, and a clever cooling system kept the building comfortable. The acoustical plan was so successful that the central light court was amazingly quiet despite the more than one thousand workers within the great space. The building included a rooftop terrace, conservatory, library, bakery, and restaurant.

After the original executives left the company in the 1920s, it struggled. In 1945 the city gained title to the building, which had been remodeled into a department store. After years of neglect this landmark was sold for just $5,000—it had cost $4 million when completed in 1906—and was demolished to make room for a truck terminal. Nothing has been built on the site.

680 Seneca Street

Buffalo, New York

Designed in 1903

Demolished in 1950

135

CUMMINGS AND COMPANY REAL ESTATE OFFICE

In 1907, after nineteen years at a nearby location in Oak Park, Edmund A. Cummings built a River Forest branch office of his downtown real estate and loan company. This was the peak development period in the two villages, and the new location gave him greater visibility. A distinguished and generous member of the community, he had previously permitted the River Forest Golf Club (1898, 1901) and the River Forest Tennis Club (1906), both designed by Wright, to locate on this large parcel of land. Both organizations eventually moved to different sites.

The Prairie Style office was just one story, built of stucco with a hipped roof. Long garden walls topped with large urns reached in both directions, emphasizing the building's horizontality and exaggerating its size. Behind protective walls on the street facade, casement windows opened to the parklike setting on the other three sides. "We welcome all who would a home acquire," announced a sign on the wall.

Its plan was simple, with a central fireplace in the reception area, a small private office, a bathroom with a toilet (the first public facility in town), and a telephone. The building also served as the address for the River Forest Land Association. A larger, preliminary plan for the office appears to have been a prototype for Wright's Pettit Memorial Chapel (1906) in Belvidere, Illinois.

By the time Cummings died in 1922 at age eighty, he had created and developed more than two hundred subdivisions in his fifty-three years in the real estate business. The parcel where his office rested was never subdivided but was sold to the Cook County Forest Preserve in 1921 to be used for its offices and a park. In 1925 Cummings's office was demolished and a hemispherical bandstand, not designed by Wright, was erected north of the original office site in his honor, using money he had left for a community improvement. Consisting of a shell over the stage with dressing rooms beneath, it was used for outdoor plays and concerts for many years. It is now a ruin, its roof removed and the dressing rooms sealed.

138

Lake Street at Harlem

Avenue

River Forest, Illinois

(top right)

Designed in 1905

Demolished in 1925

PEBBLES AND BALCH SHOP

The Pebbles Company, a pioneering business in Oak Park, began selling paint and wallpaper in 1868 from a two-story frame building just east of Harlem Avenue on Lake Street. Its business grew as the community grew, and in the early 1880s it moved down the street to a newer brick building, where it eventually added window treatments, furniture, floor coverings, lighting fixtures, and accessories to its inventory. In 1906, soon after Wright's first trip to Japan, he was hired to redesign the storefront and remodel the interior. The construction permit noted that the job cost $500.

The new storefront introduced a Japanese screen–like feeling. Above the front display window a ribbon of clerestory windows invited natural light to enter far into the shop. The horizontal band on the facade continued inside, creating a human scale suitable for the display of home furnishings. Oak cabinets were placed perpendicular to the side walls of the shop, their rectilinear shapes creating nooks for storage and display of product samples.

The Pebbleses were family friends of the Wrights. The store's founders, the brothers A. W. and S. E. Pebbles, died in 1898 and 1905 respectively. Their brother Frank was an artist not involved in the shop, but his son, Frank Jr., a contemporary of Wright, had joined his uncles in 1896. Under his management the decorating shop took pride in looking at a house from an artistic, not just a commercial, point of view. Oscar Balch, who was a partner briefly at the time of the remodeling, left the firm in 1908 but hired Wright to design his own house in 1911.

By the mid-1930s the F. M. Pebbles Company had moved to a new location at 1126 Westgate. Bramson's, a women's clothing business, moved into the old space and retained some of the improvements for a few years. It also commissioned Wright to remodel the store to suit its business, but the project was never completed. The building was replaced with a new concrete structure in the 1950s.

1107 Lake Street

Oak Park, Illinois

(bottom left)

Designed in 1907

Demolished before 1942

BRoWNE'S BookSToRE

The first of three commercial spaces that Wright designed in Chicago's Fine Arts Building was completed in 1907 as a bookstore for Francis Fisher Browne and his family, founders of the *Dial*, a conservative literary journal that objected to the experimental writing styles popular at the time. Avery Coonley, who was another Wright client that year, served on the magazine board with his brother John.

The building had originally been a Studebaker carriage factory and showroom but was remodeled in the 1890s into a ten-floor shopping center for artistic and literary goods and services. Next door to Adler and Sullivan's Auditorium Building of 1890, it was occupied by sculptors, painters, musicians, writers, publishers, decorators, and art galleries and was home to societies such as the Literary Club, Caxton Club, and Women's Club. Wright briefly had a studio there in 1908 and 1910.

The concept for the bookstore was to create a homey atmosphere combining "the best features of a well-equipped bookstore with those of a choice home library." The long, narrow space, inconveniently located on the seventh floor, was cleverly divided into nooks and alcoves created by built-in Prairie Style oak cabinets. Leather-covered seats lining the wall and leather-covered oak chairs around small tables invited visitors to sit down and make themselves comfortable. The coziness of the cubicles was enhanced by warm wood tones yet lightened by the cream-colored walls, ceiling, and magnesite floor. Atop a pier, branches of autumn leaves reached from a large geometric copper urn like the one Wright designed in 1899 for the Wallers, his prominent River Forest clients. A statue of Nike and art glass windows, some offering a lake view, recalled features of the 1895 playroom in Wright's own Oak Park home. Brass light fixtures suspended from the wood-banded ceiling were built of square panels of white glass, and quotations adorned the wall.

Within two years the store moved many of the furnishings to a more accessible space on the ground floor and then closed in 1912. The space was probably redecorated for a new tenant by that time and is now an architect's office.

Fine Arts Building

410 South

Michigan Avenue

Suite 706

Chicago

Designed in 1907

Demolished in 1912

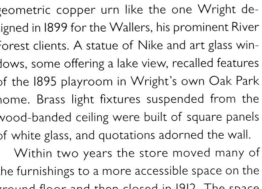

THURBER ART GALLERY

Fine Arts Building

410 South

Michigan Avenue

Fifth Floor

Chicago

(top right)

Designed in 1909

Demolished probably

by 1917

142

Occupying the entire fifth floor of the Fine Arts Building, the W. Scott Thurber Art Gallery sold American and foreign paintings, watercolors, and prints and did framing and art restoration. After designing the space in 1909, Wright received plaudits in the February 1910 issue of *International Studio* magazine, which noted that the gallery was admirably refined and combined Japanese simplicity with the ideas of the German progressives and Viennese Secessionists. Wright, said the magazine, "carefully [considered] every detail of room size and height, the lighting by day and night, the placing of doors and windows, the breaking up of the wall surfaces, the design and use of each piece of furniture, without losing sight of the minor points of utility which must of course govern the major artistic conception."

Richly crafted, the shop had white and gold magnesite floors with brass inlay, walls of gilded cork and rough plaster, and fumed oak cabinets with a bronzed finish and a white holly inlay. In colors of white, dull gray, yellow, and black, the large double-paneled, geometric, art glass skylights became the space's central focus. Because the gallery was located on the top floor of a newer addition to the building, the skylight was lighted naturally during the day and artificially at night. The golden color scheme of the shop brilliantly enhanced the artwork.

Wright, a master at designing custom cabinetry, created specialized built-in and freestanding pieces to display and store assorted works of art. As he did in other commercial spaces, he divided the room into intimate viewing areas, using dividers and screens that did not reach the ceiling so that the overall spaciousness was not lost. Tables and leather-covered stools and chairs were scattered around to add to the domestic feeling of the interior.

The family-run business continued for many years but moved to East Washington Street in 1917 and then to other locations. It is unknown how long Wright's gallery improvements remained in the Fine Arts Building, but they were probably taken out by 1917. The Harrington Institute, a design school, has occupied the space since 1962.

SToHR ARCADE SHOPS

Wright's adeptness at fitting a building to its site was challenged by the commission for a commercial development to be tucked beneath the elevated tracks of the Northwestern Railroad. The 320-by-120-foot site was oddly shaped and came with many problems, including steel posts with girders above, and required access to the train platform.

In April 1909 the trade press had reported that Peter C. Stohr, assistant to the traffic director of the Union Pacific Railroad in Chicago, had leased the triangular corner of Evanston Street and Wilson Avenue for thirty-five years. His plan was to improve the site by adding ten to fifteen stores and offices. The site was guaranteed to have good visibility and steady traffic because it was mostly beneath the Wilson station. The commuter train had connected the area to downtown Chicago since 1900 and extended north to Evanston by 1908.

Wright was thus hired in 1909 to design a building that would maximize the potential of the difficult location. In response he cleverly created a structure that was a single story beneath the tracks but that projected beyond them. Here he added two more stories, creating a visually interesting anchoring element while increasing the rentable space. The ground floor was stepped back at regular intervals, and the second level had large arched windows with an unusual glass pattern created by curved mullions. Beneath the flat, reinforced-concrete roof an air space was created above the ceiling to help muffle the sound of the trains. The three most prominent early tenants were a National Tea grocery, a large photographic studio, and W. G. Young and Company Real Estate.

The station was eventually expanded to create a new hub and service center where commuters could connect with the North Shore Interurban trains, which took them all the way to Milwaukee. To accomplish this expansion, all the buildings on the north side of Wilson Avenue between Broadway and Kenmore Streets were demolished in 1922.

856 Wilson Avenue

Chicago

(bottom left)

Designed in 1909

Demolished in 1922

ISLAND WooLEN CoMPANY DAM OBSERVATION DECK

William McFetridge was studying art in Chicago when he was called home to the family woolen mill in Wisconsin on his father's death in 1893. He took over responsibility for the buildings, grounds, and power plant while his brother Edward, a banker, assumed the leading management role. In 1913 the McFetridge Lighting Company was created and a dam constructed on the Baraboo River to provide power to the Island Woolen Company as well as to nearby houses and businesses. While no drawings have been located, it is believed that Wright designed the geometric observation platforms on the abutments where the concrete met the earthen banks.

Built of preformed concrete like the rest of the massive dam, the simple cantilevered observation slabs recalled other structures that Wright designed after his European trip in 1909–10, such as the Universal Portland Cement Pavilion (1910) (see pages 152–53) and Midway Gardens (1913) (see pages 122–25). Their only decorative elements were integral to the straightforward design and expressed in the handling of the materials. Shells from the river were inset into concrete columns, and the roof of a small shelter was anchored by chains. Railings, benches, and stairs on both sides of the river defined and celebrated the control imposed over the rushing waters and established a parklike setting.

McFetridge, a painter, land conservationist, and patriot in favor of conscription, had worked briefly as a draftsman in Louis Sullivan's office while Wright was there in 1892. In 1924 he wrote to Wright's son John that he "used to see quite a little of your father. I learned more about drawing and kindred things in a few minutes from him I think than any person I knew." As an art critic and collector, he was a useful friend to Wright in the 1920s, when the architect was forced to part with his Japanese art collection to alleviate his financial problems.

Confirming evidence for this project is lacking because of a gap in the McFetridge-Wright correspondence of this period. But the design characteristics and the client connection seem to suggest that Wright, who lived just thirty-five miles away, designed the observation deck. The mill closed in 1949, and the dam and surrounding elements were dynamited in 1972 when repairs proved too costly.

144

Second Avenue

near Ochsner Park

Baraboo, Wisconsin

Designed in 1913

Demolished in 1972

Island Woolen Mills Dam, Baraboo, Wis.

MORI ORIENTAL ART SHOP

Fine Arts Building

410 South

Michigan Avenue

Suite 801

Chicago

Designed in 1914

Demolished probably

in 1922

Wright, an avid, respected collector and dealer of Japanese prints, made his first trip to Japan in 1905, followed the next year by the first exhibition of his Japanese print collection at the Art Institute of Chicago. A frequent visitor to Japan between 1913 and 1922, he acted as an agent for others as well as buying and selling art for himself. He was also a member of the Caxton Club, located in the Fine Arts Building in Chicago, which frequently held lectures on Japanese prints that attracted collectors. Ralph Fletcher Seymour, a small specialty publisher, was also located in the building and published Wright's first book, *The Japanese Print,* in 1912. It is not surprising that through one of these connections Wright would come to know the art dealer Shigehisa H. Mori.

For many years after Wright designed a shop for Mori in 1914, the two maintained contact. Mori knew Wright's Tokyo friends Arata Endo and Aisaku Hayashi, and as late as 1944 Mori sold Wright what he described as "a masterpiece by Kiyohata who is the Harunobu of our time," adding that Wright's friend and fellow collector W. S. Spaulding owned one as well.

Little evidence remains about the shop on the eighth floor of the build-

ing, which was probably dismantled when Mori left the space in 1922. It consisted of a large, sparsely furnished display area, a conference room, an office, and storage space. Wright's drawings indicate that the areas were defined by carpets. Wall panels above the counters were of fabric mounted in wood frames, like shoji screens. They provided a practical surface on which to present various prints. Distinctive light fixtures were suspended over the display area. Oak cabinets, tables, and chairs were simple rectilinear designs, more delicate than Wright's earlier furniture.

Mori moved several times but returned to the Fine Arts Building by the 1940s—to a different space, suite 641. Some of the furnishings were later transferred to his successor and were used until 1969, when the stools, tables, and chairs were donated to the University of Illinois in Chicago. The original Wright-designed shop is now an architect's office.

BLUE PARROT PATIO TEA ROOM

1120 Westgate Street

Oak Park, Illinois

Designed in 1934

Demolished probably

by 1940

Grace Pebbles, the wife of Wright's childhood friend Frank Pebbles Jr., operated three successful dining establishments in Chicago before opening another one in 1934, located on the second floor of a new commercial building behind her husband's decorating shop in suburban Oak Park. She developed the concept of a space within the restaurant called the Celebrity Room, located in the southeast corner adjoining the larger, skylighted main room and centered around a collection of memorabilia on local residents.

Pebbles sent Wright a drawing of the room and asked for design assistance. William Beye Fyfe, a Taliesin apprentice and fellow Oak Parker, was assigned to the task. Although Wright was consulted on this project, marked up the sketches, and was paid for the work, the design was primarily Fyfe's.

This little-known and atypical effort from Wright's studio consisted mainly of a few cabinets and a wall mural for the Celebrity Room. The simple built-in cabinets housed a salad bar and serving stands that wrapped around two columns. The mural was composed of black silhouettes of Wright buildings painted on lemon-yellow walls; tan prairie grasses and abstracted sidewalks connected the images, all of which were Oak Park buildings except the un-built St. Mark's Tower, which Wright had designed in 1929 for New York City. The concept was derived from a Christmas card that Wright had admired in which Fyfe had used a silhouette of Taliesin (1911–59).

The result must have met with Wright's approval because he asked Grace Pebbles to add the Taliesin Fellowship insignia to the wall. The tea room closed after five years and was demolished probably by 1940.

147

PORTER (HEURTLEY)   UNITY TEMPLE   ST MARKS IN THE BOWERY   THOMAS   THOMAS   ROBERTS   CHENEY   GALE

EXHIBITIONS

Although most of the structures that Wright designed were intended to last more or less indefinitely, others were meant to be transitory. The real ephemera in Wright's body of work were his exhibition structures, whether designed for himself or for a client. Each was created to make a dramatic statement and serve a single purpose for only a limited period of time.

Wright, always a showman, liked to exhibit his own work and personal collections. He originated some presentations and contributed to many others. During his lifetime he participated in more than forty exhibitions, several of which traveled to numerous sites, some abroad. Recognizing that these shows were excellent selling tools, he readily adopted them as one of the many marketing strategies he needed to sustain a productive, seven-decade career. When architectural commissions were dwindling, Wright called up his communications skills to get the word out that he was still around and still had new ideas. He lectured, he wrote, and he exhibited. He encouraged photography of his work (he even retained his own photographer), had apprentices build models, created awe-inspiring drawings, and whenever possible was involved in the design and installation of the shows, even of the display fixtures. At the 1953 Usonian Exhibition in New York City (left), the architect offered almost daily guidance to the workers.

Just as all aspects of an architectural commission were important to him, each detail of an exhibition was intended to be unified, from the colors to the labels to the structural components holding and surrounding the visual presentations. Their design reflected his own changing style, Prairie Style earlier and Usonian later.

Wright's few exhibition structures were not built to endure the elements for decades or to be adapted to new uses. They were constructed quickly on temporary sites without good foundations or heating systems, used inexpensive materials, and vanished quietly. Consequently, all five examples of Wright's exhibition structures have been demolished and all other exhibits he designed dismantled. This entire category of Wright's work can now be studied only through oral histories, drawings, and photographs.

LARKIN CoMPANY PAVILION

Four years after Wright began working on its revolutionary office building in Buffalo, New York (see pages 132–37), the Larkin Company retained him to design a company exhibition structure for the Jamestown Tercentennial Exposition, the enormous fair planned to celebrate the three hundredth anniversary of the Jamestown, Virginia, settlement. The company was in its heyday, pursuing every opportunity to publicize itself and its soaps, cosmetics, and pharmaceutical items; through its factory-to-family marketing, Larkin also sold food products such as coffee and peanut butter.

The 1,500-square-foot exhibition building had two parts and was entered indirectly from two sides. The front section was a large display area for the company's 165 products and its premiums, advertised as "gifts." In 1893 customers ordering $10 worth of soap received a Chautauqua lamp valued at $10; by 1907 these premiums, which contributed to the rapid growth of the business, numbered 1,162 and included kitchen wares and clothing in addition to household furnishings. In the individual booths and display cases surrounding the space, people could see the variety of available items in room settings. A theater space toward the rear of the structure was used to show films and stereopticon views of the Buffalo area and the manufacture of the Larkin products.

Tall banner poles, part of the exterior design, added a festive air to the symmetrical, flat-roofed, plaster-and-wood building sitting among the colonial structures of the exhibition. A trolley line ran past the building, connecting it to other pavilions.

The fair was held some forty miles from the original Jamestown settlement and was open from April through November 1907. The peak attendance at the Larkin exhibit—nearly four thousand visitors—occurred on July 4. The fair was not considered a success, although Wright's pavilion received the exposition's gold medal for design excellence. In 1917 the land was sold to the U.S. Navy to create the Norfolk Naval Base. Most of the buildings were moved or demolished, but some of the larger, state-sponsored structures behind the Larkin pavilion became officers quarters and are still part of the base.

150

Powhatan Street at

Dale Street

Norfolk, Virginia

Designed in 1907

Demolished probably

by 1917

UNIVERSAL PoRTLAND CEMENT EXHIBITION

Wright's small contribution to the 1910 New York Cement Show—more a sculpture than a building—was a salute to concrete, a material that had fascinated him for many years. Plentiful and thus inexpensive, it was durable and strong, fireproof as well as waterproof, plastic and malleable, monolithic or cast into shapes and patterns. In 1928 Wright wrote an article for *Architectural Record* praising concrete's attributes and calling it "the secret stamina of the physical body of our new world." This cement show was organized by the Cement Products Exhibition Company, whose president was employed by the Universal Portland Cement Company in Chicago.

Madison Square Garden

New York City

Designed in 1910

Demolished in 1910

Portland cement is actually the binder for most structural concrete and consists basically of hydraulic calcium silicate and calcium sulfate. Various aggregates are then introduced to create different textured concretes. According to the specifications for this project, the castings were made of "fine screened birds eye gravel in smooth forms—all gravel cleaned off."

The use of concrete had grown dramatically in the first decade of the century, and with this design Wright demonstrated that the material was not just structural but highly decorative as well. In this exhibit he paired it with dark green marble for the tabletop and floor tiles. Pink, green, and white unglazed tiles were specified to be inset into the concrete, giving the sculpture the appearance of a fanciful park feature with shallow planters and a long bench. The exhibit was dismantled within the year.

Stylistically this project, designed just after Wright's return from Europe, seems to reflect some of the abstract work he saw there. The playful use of rows of tiny squares as edging and linear components foreshadowed details of Midway Gardens (1913) (see pages 122–25), the Imperial Hotel (1915–23) (see pages 126–29), the Bogk house (1916) in Milwaukee, and Hollyhock house (1917) in Hollywood, California. Vertical pylons, common elements in many of Wright's small horizontal projects, provided added stature as well as a counterpoint to the dominant theme.

WoMEN'S BUILDING

Wright's maternal relatives, the Lloyd Jones clan, were respected citizens of the Spring Green community and active in most progressive civic endeavors. When the Inter-County Fair Association opened its new Fairview Park in 1905, the Rev. Jenkin Lloyd Jones, Wright's uncle, delivered the opening address and Grace Lloyd Jones, the wife of his cousin Richard Lloyd Jones, directed the musical. The fair had originated in 1904 as a regional horse show but soon moved to a forty-acre location south of town that provided a more spacious site for tents, exhibit buildings, a baseball diamond, and a race track. When a Women's Building was proposed in 1914, it was convenient to ask Wright, who was living nearby at Taliesin, to design it.

In July the local newspaper announced that the building would be erected at the fairgrounds, and it published a design by Wright. It was to be operated by the Neighborhood Club, a group meant for men and women "who are interested in the improvement of Spring Green and its neighborhood." The Lend a Hand Club, whose members included several Lloyd Jones women, including his sister Jane Porter, was also asked to participate. But in August, a month before the fair was to open, tragedy struck the community when Wright's lover, Mamah Borthwick Cheney, her two children, and four others were killed by a deranged employee at Taliesin and the house was ravaged by fire. This devastating event has obscured the history of the construction of the fair building, which was unlike the published design yet appears to be from Wright's studio.

The simple pavilion, which was erected in time for the fair in September, had rough wooden sides, a dirt floor, a large fenced play area, and a gabled roof accented with the vertical spires that Wright liked. Here children contributed their artwork, penmanship, map drawing, and pressed flowers. Women exhibited their cooking, gardening, and needlework skills. Movable wooden partitions were covered with burlap to accommodate displays promoting various social causes. Despite his personal loss, Wright still fulfilled his promise to display his oriental art collection at the fair that year. Jane Porter organized the exhibit.

In 1920 the Fair Association voted to sell the property. The Village of Spring Green purchased it in 1924, demolished the buildings, and created a municipal golf course on the site.

Inter-County

Fairgrounds

Highway 23

Spring Green,

Wisconsin

Designed in 1914

Demolished in 1924

USONIAN EXHIBITION PAVILION AND HOUSE

In January 1951 a major exhibition of Wright's work, *Frank Lloyd Wright: Sixty Years of Living Architecture,* was previewed in Philadelphia before opening in Florence, Italy. A response to communist propaganda, it was intended to illustrate the freedom of expression possible in a democratic society. The exhibit emanated from a meeting between the U.S. ambassador to Italy, Clare Booth Luce, and the visiting businessman Arthur Kaufmann, both of whom deplored the anti-American attitude there. The show was reportedly the largest architectural exhibition devoted to one person and included eight hundred original drawings, photomurals, and models. Oskar Stonorov of Philadelphia, curator of the exhibit, worked closely with Wright and the Taliesin apprentices.

The exhibition met with enthusiasm in Italy and traveled to Switzerland, France, Germany, Holland, and Mexico City before returning to the United States two years later. The eighty-four-year-old architect received broad acclaim as he traveled to visit the various sites.

To house the exhibit in New York City when it was shown there in 1953, Wright designed a pavilion to be built on the future site of the Guggenheim Museum, completed in 1959. Here a team of Wright's apprentices supervised by David Henken repaired the travel-worn exhibit and assisted in constructing the shelter and a model Usonian home. Wright was on hand for most of the process, directing the complicated operation on the busy urban site.

Steel scaffold piping was used to create the framework for the rectangular pavilion (see pages 148–49). Four-by-four-foot openings were filled with Cementos-covered boards, and the roof was covered with corrugated wire glass so that natural light could flood the interior.

Adjoining the exhibition space was a 2,100-square-foot, two-bedroom house designed to tour as part of the show. Built to illustrate Wright's Usonian house style, it was primarily of brick and plywood and was constructed on a square module. The design exemplified his ideas for moderately priced housing for the middle class. Large windows opening from the living-dining space to the terrace allowed light to pour in, expanding the space, while interior lighting was recessed in the wooden ceiling panels. Simplicity was the key: ornament was limited to simple manipulation of the building materials, and the building's rectilinear simplicity was repeated in the modular furniture designed by Wright. The house's efficiency and unity impressed the thousands who visited it before it was disassembled in February 1954.

1071 Fifth Avenue

New York City

Designed in 1953

Dismantled in 1954

LOS ANGELES EXHIBITION PAVILION

After it left New York City, the *Sixty Years of Living Architecture* exhibition moved on to Los Angeles in 1954. There Wright designed a pavilion to house the exhibit adjoining his Hollyhock house (1917) on Olive Hill, which by then was owned by the City of Los Angeles. The structure was located downhill on the east side of the dog kennels that ran from the garage to the pool.

Wright's son Lloyd had converted some of the Hollyhock bedrooms into a gallery, where the model of Broadacre City, Wright's 1934 vision for a decentralized American community, was displayed. The model for Butterfly Bridge (1947), proposed for the Wisconsin River near his home, sat on a mirror in the pool, and inside were the Guggenheim Museum (1959) and Price Tower (1952) models. A covered walkway connected the house to the new exhibition structure, which was built of steel scaffold piping and 1½-inch-thick Cementos-covered panels like the New York structure. Because of building codes in this earthquake-prone area, the pipes had to be welded together. They were painted coral, and the connecting purlin cleats were painted red. Translucent plastic panels in the ceiling allowed diffused light into the space.

The pavilion was a long, narrow building with small side galleries and a lecture room at the end. It was open to the weather on the south side and had no heating, cooling, or ventilation systems. Inscribed mottoes punctuated the surfaces. John Geiger, the Wright apprentice assigned to the project, recalls that the day before the show opened, Wright arrived to say that the entrance must be moved. A new pad was poured just hours before the first guests arrived.

Ken Ross, curator of the municipal art collection, was instrumental in bringing the Wright show to Los Angeles and used it as a stepping stone to promote a permanent art gallery. Three months after the Wright exhibition closed, the structure opened as the Municipal Art Gallery and was used until a new space, still standing, was built on Olive Hill. Despite its temporary purpose, Wright's pavilion stood for fifteen years.

4808 Hollywood

Boulevard

Hollywood, California

Designed in 1954

Demolished in 1969

ALTERATIONS

The architectural integrity of the more than four hundred surviving Wright creations varies from building to building. Some Wright-designed structures that still stand—and thus are technically not "lost"—have nonetheless been compromised by alterations so drastic that they are no longer recognizable as Wright's.

Six summer houses designed by Wright in Michigan have not fared well in their battles between property owners' changing tastes, modern lifestyles, deferred maintenance, economic realities, and preservation goals. As a group, seasonal vacation properties such as the Joseph Bagley house (1916) in Grand Beach, Michigan (left), are one of the most vulnerable types of structure, primarily because they are out of sight, off the beaten path, and beyond the reach of the most powerful preservation tool: local oversight. Rustic amenities and defects such as inadequate plumbing, poor foundations, and limited insulation complicate their care and long-term viability.

Exterior changes to historic buildings are easy to detect; interior alterations, although more difficult to see, are somewhat easier both to understand and to rectify. In the Michigan houses on the following pages (shown in their original forms), visible changes range from different exterior materials and altered rooflines to removal of windows and additions that changed the original building shape. On the inside, walls, furniture, lighting fixtures, and moldings have been lost over the years.

The two clusters of Michigan summer homes also include examples of Wright's work that have been sympathetically maintained and rehabilitated: one of the Gale cottages (5324 South Shore, Whitehall), the George Gerts double cottage (5260 South Shore, Whitehall), and the Vosburgh residence (46208 Crescent Road, Grand Beach). In the unaltered houses, the facades remain unchanged and original building materials have been respected even though some modifications have been made over the years in an effort to modernize. Like them, most of the private residences designed by Wright have been cared for as living works of art, becoming richer and more beautiful with age.

GALE CoTTAGES

For the successful realtor, land speculator, and attorney Thomas Gale and his wife, Laura Robeson Gale, Wright had designed a modified Queen Anne–style house in Oak Park, Illinois, in 1892. The idea for a Michigan vacation compound on White Lake, near Lake Michigan, arose as early as 1896, when the Oak Park newspaper announced that Wright was designing a small resort there. Wright's drafting board actually produced a vacation house for the Gales and later three rental cottages for Laura Gale that were built after her husband's death in 1907. Near his own house in Oak Park, Wright also designed for her a rectilinear, flat-roofed, stucco-and-wood house in 1909.

The Gales invested in the lakeside property jointly with Walter Gerts, who was to build a Wright cottage nearby (see page 165). The White Lake area in fact was referred to in the Oak Park newspaper as "almost a complete Oak Park annex" because many local families participated in the yachting races there. The Gales' development, known as Birch Brook, was accessible from Chicago by Lake Michigan steamers. The first Gale cottage, completed in 1897, was a two-story, board-and-batten structure with a shallow, hipped roof. It had four bedrooms upstairs and a large living room and kitchen downstairs. A generous porch extended the space into the natural setting. Its woodsy simplicity foreshadowed other recreation structures Wright designed after the turn of the century. The later rental cottages were similarly designed but had flat roofs like the one pictured at top right.

The Gale family continued to use the original house until 1961. Over the years new siding replaced some of the boards and battens, the building was moved to make room for another house, and it was then remodeled. It is now barely recognizable as a Wright design.

Two of the rental cottages have also been altered in an attempt to save them by "modernizing." Because they were seasonal, they had no running water or electricity when built and thus became obsolete in their original form, but their economic salvation resulted in their aesthetic demise.

164

5318, 5370, and 5380

South Shore Drive

Whitehall, Michigan

(top right)

Designed in 1897

and 1909

Severely altered

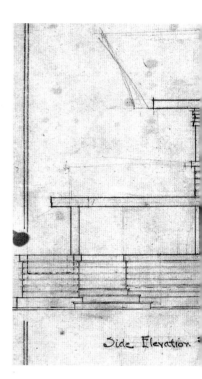

Side Elevation

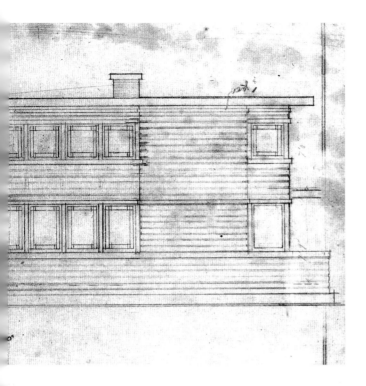

WALTER GERTS CoTTAGE

The Gerts and Gale families were relatives, neighbors, loyal Wright patrons, and prominent citizens of Oak Park and River Forest, Illinois. Both families built their summer houses on adjoining land on White Lake. Walter Gerts, who worked with his father, George, a successful brush manufacturer in Chicago, was married to Ethel Robeson, a concert violinist who was Laura Gale's sister. In 1902 Wright provided a design for Ethel and Walter Gerts's vacation house, which was built next door to his father's summer retreat, a double cottage complete with a bridge over a meandering creek, designed by Wright earlier the same year.

The Walter Gerts cottage was a single-story, dark-stained, board-and-batten structure with a hipped roof that resembled Wright's River Forest Golf Club (1898, 1901) (see pages 106–7). It was nestled quietly into its forest setting on a parcel of land owned by the two families. The front third of the building was a large veranda, which also served as the main entrance. Another porch on the back opened into the simple two-bedroom retreat. An 8½-foot-wide fireplace was the centerpiece of the open living room, which had exposed beams and a wall of windows overlooking the lake. The kitchen and maid's room were in the rear.

None of the original rustic charm remains today. The cottage has been reoriented, re-sided, and totally remodeled inside. The nearby George Gerts cottage has a second-story addition, but the original portions have been rehabilitated and remain an enchanting example of Wright's "forest houses."

In 1906 Walter and Ethel Gerts asked Wright to design a house for them in Glencoe, Illinois, with a unique plan, including a large second-floor music room, but it was never built. Wright did a minor remodeling of their River Forest house, designed by Charles White, in 1911. Despite their interest in Wright's work, little remains to celebrate the relationship.

5292 South Shore Drive

Whitehall, Michigan

(bottom left)

Designed in 1902

Severely altered

JOSEPH BAGLEY HOUSE

During the following decade (1910–20) another cluster of Wright-designed vacation houses was built not far from Chicago in Grand Beach, Michigan. Of the houses created for Joseph Bagley, W. S. Carr, and Ernest Vosburgh, only the Vosburgh house has been well maintained in its original form. The others have suffered from adaptations that have obscured Wright's vision.

Sited on a sandy Lake Michigan dune, the Bagley residence of 1916 was built of wood and plaster and had an unusual stepped-back, U-shaped symmetrical plan with a grassy terrace in the center, which served as a broad entry court. The living room reached out behind it, glazed on three sides, to take advantage of the panoramic view of the lake. On one side of the terrace was the bedroom wing and on the other the dining and kitchen wing.

With its Bedford limestone urns, the house was more formal and substantial than Wright's Prairie Style rural retreats of the century's first decade. In its original execution, it seemed more closely related to Taliesin (1911–59) than to Wright's earlier work. Made at a pivotal time in his career, the design incorporated new ideas absorbed during Wright's visits to Europe and Japan. Its simple planes and cleaner lines reflected a slightly different interpretation of the Prairie Style and marked a move in new directions.

Over the years additions have been made to the house, porches have been enclosed, and windows and the floor plan have been changed. The Bagley house is no longer an architecturally significant country escape but a nondescript, modernized house, its original form becoming more obscure as time passes.

166

47017 Lakeview Avenue

at Cedar Street

Grand Beach, Michigan

Designed in 1916

Severely altered

CARR HOUSE

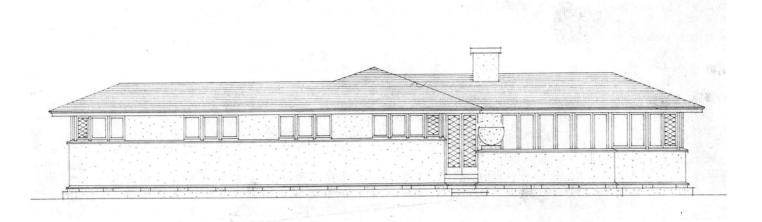

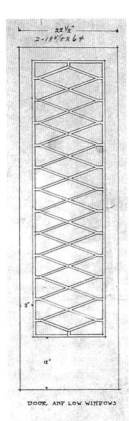

DOOR AND LOW WINDOWS

Another Chicago businessman, W. S. Carr, built his Wright-designed summer home on a bluff near the Bagley house. Sharing the more simplified and abstract late Prairie Style features of the Bagley (see page 166) and Vosburgh houses, it was constructed in 1916 of stucco over a wood frame. Like Sherman Booth's Ravine Bluffs development (1915) in Glencoe, Illinois, Wright used simple wood banding beneath ribbons of casement windows, although the Carr house was only one story.

Two staggered rectangular wings, one for living and the other for sleeping, created a horizontal residence beneath broad, hipped roofs. The four bedrooms overlooked Lake Michigan and were connected by a partially screened hallway, creating a camplike environment. The "activities room" or living space, with its central fireplace, opened on three sides to views of the lake. Screen doors led to a large terrace.

It is unknown whether the urns and diamond-paned windows Wright designed were ever completed or whether Wright was available to oversee the construction, as he was in Japan and California for such long periods during this time.

Numerous changes have been made to the house over the years. Most notably, the stucco was covered with a stone veneer. The hallway was enlarged and enclosed, as was the terrace. Rarely published, both the Bagley and Carr houses have gone virtually unnoticed by Wright students. While they may serve the present owners adequately, they no longer reveal Wright's genius or the first owners' dreams.

46039 Lakeview Avenue

near Pine Street

Grand Beach, Michigan

Designed in 1916

Severely altered